A RAGE FOR FALCONS

A RAGE FOR FALCONS

An Alliance Between Man and Bird

STEPHEN J. BODIO

Illustrated by Jonathan Wilde
Introduction by Helen Macdonald

Skyhorse Publishing

Skyhorse Publishing books may be purchased in bulk at special discounts for sales promotion, corporate gifts, fund-raising, or educational purposes. Special editions can also be created to specifications. For details, contact the Special Sales Department, Skyhorse Publishing, 307 West 36th Street, 11th Floor, New York, NY 10018 or info@skyhorsepublishing.com.

Skyhorse® and Skyhorse Publishing® are registered trademarks of Skyhorse Publishing, Inc.®, a Delaware corporation.

Visit our website at www.skyhorsepublishing.com.

10 9 8 7 6 5 4 3

Library of Congress Cataloging-in-Publication Data is available on file.

Interior design by Joe Freedman
Cover design by Jane Sheppard
Cover photo courtesy of Michael Quinton

Print ISBN: 978-1-63450-672-4
Ebook ISBN: 978-1-63450-949-7

Printed in the United States of America

To Betsy, of course,
for everything

"First the hawk, then the horse, then the hounds, then, and only then, the humble falconer."

—*Anon.*

Falconry is not a hobby or an amusement: it is a rage. You eat it and drink it, sleep it and think it. You tremble to write of it, even in recollection. It is, as King James the First remarked, an extreme stirrer-up of passions. Every falconer who reads this book will write angry and contemptuous letters to me, calculated to laud his own abilities and to decry mine.

—T. H. WHITE,
*The Godstone
and the Blackymor*

ACKNOWLEDGMENTS

I'd like to thank all the falconers and others who have helped me through the years. Ralph Buscemi deserves special mention—I was his apprentice, and learned how to do it right from him. Mark Fanning gave me Cinnamon, and Tom Ricardi bred Gremlin. Bill Satterfield, veterinarian and falconer, cured my birds when they were ill. Cornell University brought back the peregrine, and John Tobin was my project partner, telling war stories on the mountain. Harry McElroy taught me how an accipiter thinks, if "thinks" is the word, and was a gracious host in Nevada. Charles Schwartz showed me his breeding project, and told me tales of sage grouse. Jim Skidmore, master long-winger, taught me the secrets of waiting on. Kent Carnie gave me hours of good talk and valuable historical insights. Any errors or opinions in this book are mine alone; its virtues owe everything to my friends. To all the above, and all not mentioned, good hawking!

And a special thanks to Jon Wilde for the perfect illustrations, to Nick Lyons for being the kind of editor that I thought had vanished, to Ed Gray and his *Journal* for support, and to Betsy for more than typing.

Magdalena, New Mexico
1983

INTRODUCTION TO THE 2015 EDITION

When this book came out, I was twenty-two years old; a scruffy literature graduate who'd flown hawks for years. My two great loves were falconry and literature. They lived at the opposite ends of my life and barely touched. I had a vast library of falconry books, and they came mostly in two kinds: dusty antiquarian tomes or modern how-to manuals. When I bought a copy of *A Rage for Falcons* I assumed it was the latter, and opened it expecting the dry voice of the self-professed teacher. But it wasn't there. Instead, a kestrel—a 'five-ounce, helicoptering, cow-pasture bug hawk'—descended from the sky to the author's baited trap.

Blam! Reading those first few pages I was caught as fast as that kestrel and was just as surprised. For this was the real thing. It was a book by an expert falconer who could write like an angel. *A Rage for Falcons* taught me that modern falconry books could be literature, and it inspired me to try one day to write one too. This is not a book about how to train a bird of prey. It is something much rarer, richer, and better. If you've ever wondered what falconry feels like, what it is like to gain the trust of a wild hawk, train it, watch it fly, hunt and return to you, this book will show you. But be warned: it's heady stuff.

A Rage for Falcons comprehensively skewers the common assumption that falconry involves oppressing or subjecting wild birds to your will. That is not what falconry is about, and it has never been so. Back in early-modern Europe, falconry was associated with the ruling classes partly because it was expensive—back then a good falcon could cost as much as half the yearly income of a knight—but also because it was a visible display of one's ability to govern with wisdom, rather than relying on brute power to achieve your ends.

Everyone knew that a mistreated hawk would fail to fly or be lost, so a good hawk was a testament to your patience, understanding, and negotiating skills. The falconers' role, wrote seventeenth-century falconer Edmund Bert, is to provide for all your hawk's needs, and behave in ways that make your hawk love you. Wise falconers will always tell you that hawks are not pets. The end-game, writes Bodio, is always as close to wildness as possible.

* * *

What of its author? You might have come across Bodio's elegant book reviews in *Gray's Sporting Journal*, his superb books on pigeons or eagles. You might have read *Querencia*, his great and moving meditation on love and loss and home. But if Bodio is new to you, then know that the book you are holding is by one of the great modern sportsman-naturalist-writers. Soon after meeting him Annie Proulx realized that here was a man "vastly well-read in history, paleontology, archaeology, climatology, who knew about ancient horses, the history and habits of the dog, Egyptian mummification processes, could quote from Buffon, Charles Wilkes, William Bartram, Wilfred Thesiger, and the authors of little-known treatises on gyrfalcons and eagles." Bodio is all those things, and more. Sometimes he seems a visitor from the nineteenth century, a traveler from a time when a deep knowledge of literature, history, the natural world, and our intimate relation with it through hunting, observing, collecting, and animal-keeping were considered signs of rare humanity rather than eccentricities. But he is also modern as hell. Bodio might keep ancient breeds of hunting dogs and falcons, but *A Rage for Falcons* could not have been written at any other time. It is about falconry, yes. But it is also about a particular time and place in America. Suffused with the tang of sagebrush and the hush of snowy east coast woods, it reads like some wondrous hybrid of Tom Wolfe's *The Right Stuff* and Aldo Leopold's *A Sand County Almanac*.

In prose that moves from gentle informality to hell-for-leather gonzo virtuosity, Bodio vividly recollects flights and the shifting weather of forest and open country. He pleats science with history and anecdote, moving fearlessly across time and space—one moment dramatizing a hawk-trapper's set up in nineteenth-century Holland so vividly you feel you are there, the next writing with wry humor of the aching boredom of sitting in a hide in thin rain waiting for hawks that never come. He is wonderfully honest about the frustrations and difficulties of a sport that can bewilder you, horrify you, perhaps even injure you. And his raptors will never leave you. He captures not just the appearance of the different species used in falconry, but their essential moods and palpable otherness. A trapped sharp-shinned hawk "whipping around in the box in a kind of insectile fury like a predatory butterfly." A falcon ruffling her feathers to look like "a dry pine cone," or "burning low over the landscape as if she were jet-assisted."

As I grew up and learned to fly hawks in England, American falconry seemed wilder and rawer than our own. British falconers can only fly captive-bred raptors, for example, and don't use live birds to train hawks. And for much of the twentieth century, European falconers clung to the old ways of doing things, caught up in visions of falconry's lost golden age. But as Bodio observes, things were different in America. The would-be falconers who took up the sport in America in the 1920s were nature-obsessed kids "Daniel Booneing in the willow thicket below the tracks," as Aldo Leopold put it. They weren't flying hawks because they were bewitched by falconry's medieval past, but because it let them live closely with wild creatures they loved and admired. Untrammeled by tradition, they and their descendants took hidebound European falconry, shook it, and turned it into something both true to its oldest roots and also impossibly new. Bodio gives a superb history of falconry in the New World, where falconers invented radio-transmitters small enough to be carried by hunting falcons, pioneered the use of kites and balloons in training, and introduced new species like the Harris' hawk, a rangy black and chestnut avian wolf from the Southern

States, the most popular bird of prey used in falconry today. And as Bodio relates, falconers were behind the captive-breeding and reintroduction program that brought the peregrine back to American skies after the dark DDT years.

Since this book was published, UNESCO has listed falconry as a masterpiece of world intangible cultural heritage and global falconry forums have sprung up on the Internet. The number of women falconers has soared. In the Gulf States, huge hybrid falcons follow lures trailed behind model aircrafts, or engage in spectacular aerial battles with remote-controlled artificial flying houbara, their traditional prey. Falconry is a moving, living art. But whatever form it takes, that eternal bond between bird and human is at its heart. *A Rage for Falcons* is a precious celebration of that bond, and a celebration of the fact that falconry exists, still, in an age of ever-growing ecological impoverishment and increasing human disconnection from the natural world. To be a good falconer, explains Bodio, requires a feeling for the woods and fields, an intuitive grasp of ecology. And falconry is a transformative thing. It pulls you out of yourself and drags you from the human world into a wilder one. It lets you see though other eyes; develop an empathy for what Bodio calls "other bloods." As another superb modern falconer-writer, Rebecca O'Connor, explains, "you don't know wild until you've equal parts sprinted and stumbled across rough terrain chasing the terror of a lost hawk, only to pause and realize you are utterly lost. Scraped, gasping, and half-delirious, it is in this place where things happen that change your life. That is what is truly wild." Whatever comes next for falconry, it will always be one of the best ways to interact with the wild—both the wild out there, and the wildness inside ourselves. And as long as there is falconry, Bodio's book will be the best introduction to what it is, and to why some people choose to share their lives with hawks and watch them fly, their faces turned to the sky and love and wonderment in their hearts.

—Helen Macdonald

INTRODUCTION

"All in all, falconry is the perfect hobby."
—Aldo Leopold

THE MALE KESTREL checked in his flight over the pitch-pine barrens, turned into the wind, hovered for a moment, and dropped like a stone onto the tethered pet-store mouse. I waited for a moment in disbelief that such an event, so far known only in books, could be happening in real life. Then I pulled the string attached to the bow net. The clamshell contraption of badminton netting and yardsticks popped closed and I ran in to grab the tiny falcon before it could pull loose. Its high-pitched protests were like fingernails on blackboards, like breaking glass, but they could have been triumphal music. Nor did it bother me a bit when, as I grabbed the little monster's electric body, he turned on his back in terror and "footed" me with a handful of hot needles. I had pulled a hawk out of the sky.

A half hour later my friend caught his mate. A week later the male flew unrestrained across my friend's yard to me. As he placidly munched on the piece of stew beef I held between my fingers, I thought that the only thing better than pulling down a hawk from the sky by trickery was to return him there and have him come back to your call because he wanted to. Twenty years later, I still do. When, a couple of days later, the female choked

1

on an oversized hunk of meat and died, my friend's mother cut the little male loose. It was an act of kindness that I resented for a year. But the moment of contact had kindled in me a rage for falcons that will be a part of me until I die.

There is no practical reason for falconry to exist. Although it probably originated as long as four thousand years ago, it is amazing that the practice did not die out soon afterward when its first adherents starved. Probably then as now, hawking was a sort of recreation for the lucky few rather than a practical way to put meat on the table. Although the French called the goshawk "cuisinier," the only people who have ever made an economic success of falconry were the Kirghiz of central Asia. They caught foxes and even desert wolves for their skins, using monstrous golden eagles that might vent their displeasure at a missed kill on the falconer or his horse. (A couple of years ago *New Scientist* magazine published a Russian photo of two Kirghiz tribesmen that showed a wonderful combination of tradition and technology. The two hunters sit cross-legged on the ground drinking tea brewed in a solar cooker, which is flanked on one side by a hunting eagle and on the other by a pair of hairy Bactrian camels.)

Where falconry started is more a matter for scholarly debate than one of interest to the practitioner. The oil sheiks enjoy a form of hawking that, minus their custom Range Rovers with gold fixtures, is much like that practiced in the Middle Ages. The Japanese also have a long tradition of hawking that is part mirror image, part odd cultural parallel to ours. For reasons of terrain, their "noble" bird is the goshawk rather than the long-winged falcon; they use the sight of a familiar box where food is kept to call the bird rather than a bird-shaped lure. You can find ancient references to hunting with birds all across the steppes of Asia and up into the north and west as far as Scandinavia. What is certain is that the formal manners of western falconry came to

Europe through the crusades, and through such obsessed eccentrics as Emperor Frederic II, who wrote what was both the first book on falconry and the first scientific bird book.

Hawking soon rose from its obscure beginnings to become the sport of medieval Europe's aristocrats, a metaphor for war, a model for battle tactics and sometimes a substitute for them. More than one old warlord supposedly lost his decisive battle while occupied with hawk craft rather than war craft. Kings traded hawks for prisoners. Knights took hawks to church so often that churches had rules barring them, although some ranking churchmen were not above bringing in their own birds. A few couples even got married with hawks on their fists, medieval precursors to those modern couples who take their vows underwater or while skydiving.

Falconry has become so identified with this time that if anyone thinks of it today, it is in connection with jousting and tournaments and noble ladies with ice-cream-cone hats. Even the historically minded would probably date its demise to about the time of Henry VIII, who almost drowned while chasing a hawk. (His pole broke while he was vaulting a ditch and he stuck head-down in the mud.) But falconry never died out. The rising efficiency of the gun, which had no temperament, didn't eat, and didn't produce tons of droppings, put a lot of dilettantes out of business. The identification of falconry with the Stuarts and its association with old-fashioned royalist squires did not help it.

Still, it struggled on to one last short golden age in England toward the end of the eighteenth and the beginning of the nineteenth centuries. Some of the great hawking figures of that time are better known to sporting historians for their activities in such sports as racing or coursing. The most notorious falconer of the period was one Colonel Thomas Thornton, perhaps the last man until recent times to understand the gyrfalcon. He went out, according to a contemporary sporting journalist, accompanied by "fourteen servants with hawks on their wrists, ten hunters, a pack of stag-hounds and lap dog beagles, and a brace of wolves.... Two brace of pointers, and thrice as many greyhounds in rich buff and blue sheets, with armorial bearings, followed in their train." Thornton had a mistress who posed as his wife and was also a serious horsewoman, one accomplishment being considered almost as risqué as the other. He bet on her in races and engaged her competitors in public brawls in the newspapers and in the grandstand of the race track at York.

But the reign of Victoria and the spread of such vices as respectability and reared pheasant shooting conspired to make such characters seem a little primitive. Falconry did survive in England, and its practitioners seemed to enjoy it. But they narrowed its focus to the chasing of Scottish grouse with the peregrine; the few other kinds of hawking practiced were regarded as inferior. Overt enthusiasm, the splendid gyrfalcon and, above all, innovation, were banished from the sport.

The English are still fossilized. The most respected contemporary English falconry authority dismisses the gyrfalcon as a useless, if pretty, toy. S. Kent Carnie, an experienced American falconer who has hawked in Scotland, is blunt: "The Brits have nothing to teach us but history." It has taken about one hundred twenty years, a new bunch of dedicated madmen, a little bit of science and technology, and the vast public lands of the American West to give us a new golden age of falconry.

L ET ME tell you a few things that falconry is not. First, it is not pet-keeping. Most falconers cringe when some well-meaning acquaintance refers to their birds as pets. A falconer's bird, however tame and affectionate, is as close to a wild animal in condition and habit as an animal that lives with man can be. Above all, it hunts. A bird that is carried around on the fist and petted but never flown may be happy—I leave such issues to behaviorists and animal-rights advocates. But a wild animal that cannot engage in its natural behavior is barely an animal, and a pet bird is neither a falconer's bird nor even a real hawk. Nor is its owner a falconer, nor, no matter what he may tell you, is he practicing falconry.

Second, falconry is not pageantry. Some of the Creative Anachronists, that odd group of people who cluster around technical institutes pretending to be knights and bashing at each other with wooden swords, have been known to bring a tame kestrel or other docile hawk to pseudo-Renaissance Faires. A hawk's place is in the sky, not at a human festival. When hawks were always on people's fists, bringing one to a fair was not necessarily an affectation. Now it is just that.

To UNDERSTAND FALCONRY, you must understand the nature of the relationship between man and bird. Dogs are man's servants; horses, basically classy, self-willed transportation. A hawk is your master or mistress. "First the hawk, then the horse, then the hounds, then and only then the humble falconer," goes the old maxim. The education of the falconer is a chastening process during which you learn to be polite to an animal. The bird never gives an inch—you can coax it but never bully or even discipline it. Your purpose in the field is to assist the bird, your reward the companionship of a creature that could disappear over the horizon in fifteen seconds flat. And the closer your bird approaches the behavior of a wild bird the better, as long as it approves of your company.

One of the two most popular questions asked of falconers is "How do you teach it to kill?" You don't; it already knows how to kill. You teach it to return if it doesn't kill, to allow you to approach it if it does. This return is one of the great thrills of falconry. Under some circumstances it can be almost as exciting as the chase.

There are falconers in the Southwest who barely handle their birds. The birds fly into the car for a trip to the hunting grounds, fly out when they get there, and are alerted to the presence of game by whistles and hand signals. And make no mistake, despite the absence of physical contact these are, of necessity, among the tamest of falconers' birds. A few have gone even further. The old master falconer of Ireland, Ronald Stevens, kept two very tame gyrfalcons flying entirely free, calling them in when he wanted to go hunting. These birds were tame because they were captive raised. But Ralph Buscemi, a successful traditional falconer, has trained a pair of wild goshawks to receive food from his hands like sacrificial offerings. He started by tossing wild pigeons to them during a bad winter when he was afraid they would starve. Now, several years later, their tameness is startling—one will rotate over your head like a helicopter and extend a polite talon to your hand for its meat. The goshawks appear each December with the snow and soon begin to follow Ralph around the yard, perching ten feet away. "If I could get 'em to follow me in the woods, I could give up the rest of it," says Ralph.

Which still circles around the appeal, the drama, the obsession. In some sports the thrill comes from physical accomplishment, but except for such skills as hooding a recalcitrant bird, there is little of that in falconry. The falconer does not really *do* very much once he arrives in the hunting field. Not only is he servant to a bird; he is, in the words of hound writer M. H. Salmon, "accessory to the hunt." Tom Cade, founder of the Cornell peregrine program, falconer and scientist, argues that falconry is a highly evolved version of bird watching. This rings true, yet does not go quite far enough. Recently I was talking to S. Kent Carnie, who quoted Alvah Nye, dean of American falconry, on the matter. Nye stated his thesis in four words: *"You are the bird."*

It seems to say more than any other explanation. As your bird soars, dives, rolls, chases, and strikes, you rush forward, yelling, heart beating as if it were pumping blood to those incredible wings. You experience an extreme form of the hunter's sensation described by Aldo Leopold: "The man who does not like to see, hunt . . . or otherwise outwit birds and animals is hardly normal." Or maybe T. H. White's blunter summation is better: "Blood lust is a word which has got shop soiled. They have rubbed the nap off it. But split it into its parts, and think of Lust."

Falconry is still White's "mania." In the last twenty years the peregrine first declined because of exposure to pesticides, then benefited from the most intense and successful restoration effort ever given any bird—an effort sparked and carried out almost *entirely by falconers.* During the same time span, there have been such incidents as the attempted purchase (by check, on the spot, by an Arab government official) of the Air Force's white gyrfalcon mascot, for twenty-five thousand dollars. The last decade has seen arctic Indians and oil-company helicopter pilots ripping off North Slope eyries, grand-jury investigations of prominent falconers, intense political lobbying by pro- and anti-falconry factions, and an amount of venomous personal conflict that has little to do with biological realities. People have risked stable careers in order to smuggle falcons, marriages to fly them, fortunes to breed them. I myself have been questioned by federal agents, and a couple of years ago I got a letter from the editor of a national scientific publication accusing me and people like me of causing the imminent extinction of all birds of prey. Is it any wonder that James I called hawking "an extreme stirrer-up of passions"?

THIS BOOK will offer a subjective look at modern American hawking, and the pragmatic romantics who practice it, by a writer who is also a falconer. It is not a treatise or a scholarly report, and above all, it is not a how-to book for the hawking enthusiast. It is a report from the sagebrush basins and the shortgrass plains, the farm lots and the breeding barns. It will contain some science and natural history and I hope a little poetry. But finally, telling you *why* someone would practice falconry is trying to catch the prairie wind in a box. Hunting in this society is a game. It is a superior sort of game, and a life-and-death game with echoes of our evolutionary past, but it is still a game, not a primitive way of earning a living. In such highly developed games as falconry or fly fishing, the ritual and intricacies of the sport are at least as important as the catch; in such intricacies lies much of their appeal. In my first ten years of hawking, mostly for rabbits and pheasants, I caught a fair number of rabbits and very few pheasants. I also caught a feral house cat (it broke away without injuring itself or the hawk), a couple of mice, a frozen half-rabbit, and, in the vast majority of cases, nothing at all.

In *The Goshawk*, White said in defense of the time he spent training a hawk:

> These efforts might have some value because they were continually faced with the difficulties which the mind had to circumvent, because falconry was a historic though dying sport, because the faculties exercised were those which throve among trees rather than houses, and because the whole thing was inexpressibly difficult.

All the old anachronistic field sports—archery, fly fishing, coursing, hunting with primitive weapons—partake somewhat of these characteristics. They are traditional and replete with ritual; they are more difficult and somehow more natural than their technology-dependent counterparts. They demand rapport with "other bloods," knowledge of land, water, and air. What starts as fun may become a way of life; more than one falconer has moved his family from the security of the crowded East to the empty plains just for the sake of what novelist Thomas McGuane called (speaking of trout rather than of birds) "not even a mammal!"

And some continue to take that one step farther. A friend delights to tell of the time he devastated a couple of canvassing Jehovah's Witnesses by taking them to where his proud peregrine sat on her perch and announcing, "This is what I worship." You may say he goes too far, yet it is not that rare an attitude. Another friend put it explicitly. He had called about a rumored anti-falconry bill. "Man," he said, "they can't do that." He paused for a moment, as if I didn't see the horror clearly enough. "I mean," he continued, "it's like they're messing with my *religion!*"

1

"What but fear winged the birds, and hunger
Jeweled with such eyes the great goshawk's head?"
—Robinson Jeffers

M OST PEOPLE ASSUME there is a single savagely predatory
hawk nature. This is not true. Falconry makes use of three
main groups of diurnal predatory birds with personalities as
different as, say, cats, dogs, and bears. By the old European
terminology the three groups would be called falcons, hawks,
and buzzards. However, with typical puritan townsmen's ignorance of nature, our first colonists called all three groups "hawks,"
so that the noble peregrine became the "duck hawk" and our
commonest buzzard, the "red-tailed hawk." And just to keep
everything good and confusing they gave the name "buzzard" to
our vultures, thereby permanently tainting the word.

Still, there are several characteristics that all birds of prey
share, whether they are related or not. The first is the importance
of eyes. In birds of prey the two eyes together weigh more than
the brain; if you dissect a hawk, each eye looks as large as the
brain. Cynics and falconers alike might agree that this ratio
shows the relative importance of eyes and brain to a hawk. In
each eye of a hawk are two foveas or areas of sensitivity; a human
has one in each. Ornithologists think that one fovea in each eye
is adapted to search, and one to pursuit. Humans have two

hundred thousand cells to each square millimeter of fovea, hawks, upward of a million. The practical result is that hawks can see much finer detail than we are capable of.

Hawks also have a wider field of vision than humans do—binocular vision in front and expanded side vision that takes in everything but a narrow field directly behind—and a gyroscopic mechanism that allows the hawk to keep its head steady while its body rocks in the air currents. In controlled experiments falcons have come in to a handkerchief waved a mile away, and most falconers can tell tales of birds who responded instantly to a signal while out of sight straight overhead.

The second things all birds of prey have in common is a kind of sexual dimorphism opposite to that of most mammals. In all species of birds of prey, from parakeet-sized kestrels to golden eagles, the female is conspicuously larger than the male. Often the size difference is about one-third—perhaps the origin of "tiercel" for the male falcon. Traditionally, falconry reverses the sexual stereotypes. The females are considered strong and calm; the males swift and edgy and emotional. The Arabs, who do not see hawks breeding, have always considered the males to be females and vice versa. One distinguished diplomatic visitor to the Cornell peregrine breeding project had to be shown both mating and egg-laying birds before he dared believe the heresy of the larger female. This respect for the female sex in falconry also means that a falcon of unknown sex is as inevitably female as a ship.

The third trait shared by most hawks is less important, but woth mentioning to avoid confusion. Most hawks start out in life with a coat of feathers of a certain color which they keep for a year. At their first molt, the color changes, usually with the onset of sexual maturity. After this the hawk will molt each year, but stay more or less the same color. Some birds which delay sexual maturity until four or five years of age, like eagles, also have a number of intermittent plumage changes before the final phase. Birds in the first year are known as "eyases" until they leave the nest, or eyrie, and "passage hawks" or "passagers" from the subsequent migration or passage. Birds in adult plumage are called "haggards" if wild-caught at that stage, or "intermewed" from mewing or molting, if they have achieved the first molt in captivity.

The first group, the true falcons, has always included the choicest birds in the West. (The Japanese prefer goshawks.) In the Middle Ages no commoner could own a true falcon, and despite the disclaimers of their owners, a bit of this attitude persists to this day. In the American West, where I live, native falconers can use the prairie falcon, but unless you have a friend who is a breeder, or are the head of an OPEC nation, you are unlikely to possess a peregrine or a gyrfalcon.

Falcons were considered so desirable that the popular name for the sport of hunting with birds comes from them; "hawking" ranks a poor second. Nowadays nobody but a slightly precious recusant would call one who flies goshawks an "austringer"; *any* bird trainer is a falconer. (The same person might insist on restricting "falcon" to the female peregrine, as was proper in the Middle Ages; this would leave us without any inclusive word for the falcon group, and require us to use a different noun for each sex of every species.)

Of course in common ornithological parlance, hawks, buzzards, and falcons are all "hawks"; a falcon is simply a hawk of the genus *falco*. These birds—true falcons, or to falconers sometimes "longwings"—evolved as masters of the long chase and the power drive. They catch their prey in the air. Falcons have the triangular-tipped wings common to all the open-country coursing birds like pigeons and doves and shorebirds. They are bullet-headed and streamlined. A fifth of their weight is contained in the deep muscular breasts that drive the wings. Although like most birds they are hollow-boned and built mostly of feathers and air sacs, a given falcon will outweigh a true hawk that appears the same size. Because of this they have almost given up soaring—their heavy bodies and narrow, beating wings deliver speed, but are not as efficient for lift.

Ornithologists consider falcons to be rather distantly related to the other diurnal birds of prey, if they are related at all. Some of the more radical ones even hint at affinities with owls and parrots. To my innocent eyes the only sure thing that falcons, owls, and parrots have in common is their oddly anthropomorphic habit of holding their food up to their mouths in one foot as they nibble. But they *are* different from other raptores. Apart from easily enumerated characteristics like pointed wings, dark eyes, and a notch or "tooth" in the bill, there is an indefinable "falcon-ness" about the whole group—an alert, head-bobbing intelligence and an upright, chunky silhouette that all falcons from the four-ounce male kestrel to the four-pound female gyrfalcon seem to share.

A falcon on the perch or fist seems trusting and doglike. But to see a falcon at rest is like seeing a sleeping greyhound or a standing cheetah. The running animals look a little ungainly, with overly long toothpick legs, boat-keel chests and tucked up bellies. Similarly a sitting falcon looks a little heavy, with broad shoulders and a round parrot face. Her killing talons will be, more likely than not, tucked under her long, fluffy belly feathers. But watch her wake up. She will ruffle her feathers until she looks like a dry pine cone and shake them down with a brisk rustle—"rousing" in the apt Elizabethan parlance of falconry. She'll stretch, delicately drop a dollop of liquid "hawk chalk," and lean forward, holding her perch, rowing the air.

And then she'll leap into the air, to be transformed instantly from a kind of overgrown parakeet into something as swift and deadly and efficient as a leopard or a dragonfly or an F-16.

Suddenly she is burning low over the landscape as if she were jet-assisted. If she is an experienced falconer's bird she will work the wind, racing down and then climbing up into it, pulling hard, making great circles, higher and higher, until she reaches her "pride of place." Falcons by inclination and training "wait on" for their prey, hanging in the breeze hundreds, or even thousands, of feet above the falconer's head. An experienced bird may stand in the air for as much as half an hour. If she finds still air, she will circle, alternating flapping and short glides. If she has a head wind, she will dive, then soar up, dive and soar, riding an aerial roller coaster with what must be pleasure.

When the quarry—in falconry perhaps a duck, pigeon, prairie grouse, or pheasant, but usually a bird—breaks cover, the hawk folds its wings and drops toward the ground in a "stoop," the vertical dive that can knock a mallard out of the sky with the force of a three-inch magnum shell. Sometimes the falcon will start the stoop flying, adding the force of its own muscles to the deadly pull of gravity. Sometimes the stooping bird spirals like a corkscrew. Her head-down silhouette resembles that of an inverted valentine heart. If she is wearing bells, the rush of wind through the bell slots makes a scream audible for more than half a mile. Certainly nothing in nature looks so fast and inevitable.

Although it is not. Often she misses, and if she does, the game will most likely be over there and then. Most of the traditional quarry for true falcons can outfly the hawk in a tail chase, especially if the hawk must first recover from her stoop. But if she does hit her prey, she will flatten out, slamming past and through in an explosion of feathers rather than staying with the quarry; at two hundred miles per hour a glancing blow is safer to deal. Even then the quarry is often struck dead in the air with a broken back or shattered skull—and I know of one case where both a rather small falcon and her enormous quarry, a sage grouse, fell dead together out of the air. After the first strike, the hawk will rebound like a bouncing ball in a maneuver called "tossing up" or "throwing up" from the quarry. She can then smash it again if she needs to. If the victim is dead, the hawk may "bind" to it and ride it down; if a sturdy quarry like a sage grouse or cock pheasant goes to ground to fight off its attacker, the falcon may strafe it at high speed, striking it repeatedly in long arcs like the swing of a pendulum. But sooner or later, if she has hit well the first time, she will win. She will then perch on her prey, docile and parrotlike once again, plucking feathers and stripping a few bloody mouthfuls of flesh off its neck to tide her over until the falconer arrives.

The long-winged species flown by American enthusiasts include the kestrel, merlin, prairie falcon, peregrine, gyrfalcon, and recently, various domestic hybrids. There are also a fair number of captive-bred lanners of African and Middle Eastern stock in American falconers' hands. The kestrel is a five-ounce, helicoptering, cow-pasture bug hawk, gaudy as a songbird. It is the commonest North American raptor, as likely to inhabit a city attic as an abandoned woodpecker hole in the country. Although of perfect falcon outline, with delicate pointed wings and a notched bill, it is mostly used in falconry as a sort of training bird. It can be tamed in a week and flown prettily to the lure like some combination of model airplane and butterfly, but it seems to lose what little savagery it possesses in the ease of domestic life; I have known only two kestrels that took any quarry at all, and only one that repeated the feat.* Kestrels used to be called sparrow hawks—another instance of the puritans' ineptitude in recognizing and naming wild animals. The English have a perfectly respectable kestrel, as ubiquitous in their countryside as ours is here. It is similar in appearance to our bird and shares its habit of

---

*My illustrator, Jon Wilde, takes exception to this statement; his kestrel was a consistent game hawk, and he has known others that were.

helicopter hovering and its fondness for mice and grasshoppers. But the exiled townsmen chose to call our windhover after another common British bird, a yellow-eyed miniature woodland accipiter resembling our sharp-shinned hawk.

The merlin, although the male is no heavier than the kestrel, is another story. (Except in the naming—it used to be called the "pigeon hawk," although it is identical to the European merlin.) Despite their small size, merlins have none of the apparent delicacy of kestrels; they are chunky, broad shouldered, triangular winged and very swift. Within the falcon group there is a broad and vague division, birds that use the stoop as their primary method of hunting, like the peregrine, and those even speedier birds that excel in the tail chase, such as the gyrfalcon and its tiny replica, the merlin. Oddly, although such birds seem heftier, more massive, than their relatives, the gyr and merlin are really trickier to keep. A merlin would die in a week on a beef and chicken diet that would keep a kestrel for ten years.

The merlin is one of the great historic birds of falconry. Henry VIII was chasing a merlin when he got stuck in his ditch, although the merlin was most often flown by ladies. Mary Queen of Scots flew one during her captivity. The medieval noblewoman who flew one might well have had the advantage of her brethren. Merlins are easier to train than game hawks like the peregrine, and are just as fierce in the air. A few serious fanatics still fly merlins caught "on passage" in the fall, although the bird's tiny size, starling-sized prey, and above all its annoying habit of continuing its interrupted migration after a month or two of controlled flight have all worked against its popularity. In this age of bureaucracy the last trait is the worst—the paperwork and scrutiny involved in keeping a hawk for a couple of months is daunting. Formerly one of the most elegant ways of flying hawks, and one with almost no environmental impact, was to "borrow" them from the wild for a short time during their migration. But I digress . . .

The western prairie falcon, unknown in historical times and named late enough to avoid the puritan naming curse, is the yeoman's choice of American longwingers. Found from Alberta and Saskatchewan to Mexico in still-healthy numbers, it is hardy and weather resistant, tolerating heat and cold that would kill some of the other desirable species. It is also somewhat rough and ready in appearance, with fluffy, soft feathers of brown and tan, very unlike the hard, glossy mail of the peregrine. This kind of feathering is typical of the so-called "desert falcons," a group that includes the prairie, its close relative the saker of Europe and the Middle East, the lanner, and, according to some authorities, the gyrfalcon.* Desert falcons have a general tendency toward softer plumage, shorter toes, and tail-chasing. They also have a habit, considered rather low-rent by longwingers, of catching the occasional mouse or hare, perhaps because in their harsh arid or tundra homes they can't afford to be as picky as a peregrine living in a lush temperate river valley.

Prairies, whose nests are found near such cities as Denver and Albuquerque, who perhaps because of their plebeian rodent-eating habit have never suffered a decline in numbers as a result of man's use of pesticides, who can take a range of prey from starlings to prairie grouse, would be ideal falconer's birds except for their temperament. While individual prairies can be as docile as bird dogs, the average individual contains a mixture of skittishness and aggression that would drive a novice falconer out

---

*This matter of relations and groups of species among the falcons is exceedingly complex and still the object of much study. It seems that all the falcons so far tested can produce fertile hybrids, even three-way crosses. In this they resemble, for instance, wild dogs. Although most ornithologists would not go so far as the British ornithologist Colonel Richard Meinertzhagen, who believed all desert falcons plus the gyr were one species, it would probably be best to consider all the big members of the genus *Falco* as points on a curve, with the peregrine at one end and the gyr at the other, rather than as absolutely unrelated entities. The peregrine appears most distinct, but some desert races resemble the true "desert falcons" almost as much as they do peregrines from wetter climates.

of the sport and push even a master to cut loose the worst examples. In this they seem to compare to their nearest relative, the saker, the bird of choice in Arabian falconry. And like the saker, the prairie can be as good as a falcon ever gets if you live through the first few months. The worst-tempered hawk I have ever had in my possession was a fourteen-ounce tiercel prairie: it used to fly across the yard and grab my leg. Yet one of the sweetest and deadliest game hawks I have ever seen is a female taken under the exact same circumstances.

The peregrine is still *the* falcon. It is the first bird to be so called, the "falcon gentle" of the Middle Ages. It is perhaps the handsomest of the falcons. Its build is compact and athletic, its plumage a hard, almost shiny deep blue. Its head is marked with a helmetlike cap of black or deep slate gray. The whole effect is set off by creamy white on the throat and bright yellow around the eyes and bill and on the huge bird-killing feet.

The peregrine was called "falcon gentle" as in gentleman and commoner, not in relation to its temperament. But it is in every way a gentle bird compared to the irascible prairie or the volatile gyr. An adult-caught peregrine will seem shy, but cool and even phlegmatic; she will more likely ignore the falconer than scream at him in rage. It is a little too tempting to wonder if the polite, ladylike composure of the peregrine wasn't at least as important to its popularity among the stiff-upper-lip English falconers as were its stunning stoops at red grouse. But am I the only heretic to wonder if, except for this ability, the peregrine wouldn't be a little—well, stuffy—compared to the fiery gyr?

Until recently, the peregrine was, after the lowly kestrel, the most likely bird of prey to be met with in cities, and now that persistent pesticides are under control it may become common there again. Biologically it is remarkable, being found naturally on every continent, except Antarctica, from the poles to the tropics. Races of peregrines live on the tundra, in Baja California, in Morocco, on Tierra del Fuego, and in cliffs overlooking India's remnant jungles. They also used to nest on the Hudson Palisades and on Salisbury Cathedral. They prefer cliffs over or near water and so are spread thinly over the landscape, but until man invented DDT, you could see a peregrine almost anywhere.

The spread of petrochemical poisons after World War II almost did in the peregrines of eastern North America and western Europe. The race found in eastern North America, *Falco peregrinus anatum* (or duck hawk, to the colonial-name fan), was particularly hard hit. Within twenty years it disappeared entirely from over two hundred known eyries. An eleventh-hour ban on the persistent hydrocarbons and the quixotic dedication of the peregrine recovery team have given us back some sort of peregrine, if not quite the original *anatum*. England's birds were not so far gone. They have repopulated many of their historic eyries all by themselves.

The incomparable gyrfalcon is sometimes considered the largest and most northerly of the desert falcons and sometimes to be absolutely unique. As in so many areas of natural history and evolutionary biology, the truth is relative. The gyr has the fluffy plumage of the desert falcons, only more of it. She can cover her feet with her belly feathers when she sits upright. She has short toes and will eat fur. Some high-latitude sakers and low-latitude Asian gyrs resemble one another. But gyrs are *huge*. The females weigh as much as small eagles, the males (gyrkins or jerkins), more than most female peregrines. The author of *Falconry in Arabia*, Mark Allen, describes the gyr as being "of a size to kill a saker, one in each foot." The gyr's massiveness makes her look hulking and small-headed. She comes in all colors from nearly black through browns and grays and a kind of "chain-mail" pattern, to almost pure white. The gyrfalcon may also have some odd adaptations to polar life; the British Columbia naturalist Frank Beebe believes that gyrs may bury themselves in the snow during prolonged blizzards and have evolved some physiological adaptations such as a modified foot for lying down, and even the ability to hibernate.

Such theories still need investigation. What is certain is that gyrs are large enough to handle any conceivable falconer's prey, including five-pound sage grouse. Some of the old falconers flew them at eagles and other birds of prey, which gyrs seem to possess a natural antipathy toward, perhaps in reaction to competition on their arctic breeding grounds. Some falconer's gyrs will seek out and kill wild redtails and other slow-moving hawks, to the distress of their owners. The speed and persistence of the gyrfalcon is awesome. It can fly down a canvasback in a five-mile tail chase, and blow away, in level flight, any peregrine that ever lived. Gyrs have the furnace metabolism of the high-speed predator, burning the equivalent of a pigeon a day or more in captivity, bouncing off the walls when they are not flown on time. One I knew from the North Slope flew through trees when chasing pigeons, showering twigs over the landscape. Yet oddly, they are among the tamest of all birds used in hawking—not just the captive-bred babies, but even the wild-caught adults. It is not unusual to see a newly trapped gyr feed on the fist minutes after it is taken from the net. They are as playful as puppies or otters. And, as the reverse side to this coin, they are easily made hysterical.

The English are still peregrine partisans, and very dubious about the gyr. But in America, where the toughest tests and the potential for the finest flights now exist, the gyr and gyr crosses are crowding the peregrine as the hawk of choice. Gyrs are not natural waiters-on or stoopers, although they can be taught. In Europe, where even the most open country is smaller than the public lands of the west and is in any case privately owned, a falcon that waits on very precisely is not only desirable but necessary, and it may well take a couple of seasons for the intelligent but self-willed and slow-developing gyr to learn its business. Most contemporary European falconers are therefore unwilling to fly the gyr, with the notable exception of Ireland's innovative Ronald Stevens.

The more common attitude toward the gyr in England is exemplified by Philip Glasier, who runs the Falconry Centre at Newent in Gloucestershire. In *Falconry and Hawking* as recently as 1978, he stated that "past and present records would indicate that gyrs are rather disappointing birds from the falconer's point of view." His predecessor Colonel Thornton might have been surprised at this news. He chased hares for the pot, and kites—high-flying scavenger hawks—for the sheer thrill, with the same individual gyrs. And kites at least were among the most difficult game ever to be taken by trained hawks, possessing both stamina and the ability to climb faster even than the gyr because of their light wing-loading. But between 1800 and the present, England was cut up and enclosed, and the huge parties that were spread over the land to spot for the gyr's long chases became prohibitively expensive. The English turned to grouse hawking, control, and pretty stoops. Only recently, on the sagebrush-desert public range of the American West, has the gyr come into its own again. With the Bureau of Land Management tracts standing in for private estates, electronic beepers for the field of retainers, and the mighty sage hen for the Scottish red grouse, a few North American falconers are combining the best of classical hawking and the mightiest falcon of all in a whole new game.

Two other longwings deserve brief mention. The lanner is a desert falcon found throughout Africa, the Middle East, and Southeastern Europe. While it is often compared to the prairie falcon it looks more like a small peregrine with softer feathering. Its handsome adult plumage, blue gray on the back with a reddish cap and cream colored belly, resembles that of the desert

peregrines; its immatures look oddly like young arctic peregrines, though with duller, softer feathers. Its personality is far
more amenable than a prairie's or a saker's; lanners are usually
very tame and intelligent, though anthropomorphic falconers
often complain about their "laziness." Maybe they're just too
smart to work hard. Lanners are also fairly easy to breed, so there
are more of them being flown in North America than any other
exotic hawk.

The other longwing of importance in North America is that
nebulous entity, the hybrid. Of course there is no single hybrid—
there are peregrine/gyr-falcon crosses, peregrine/prairie crosses,
gyr/merlins, and even peregrine/prairie/merlins. Hybrids deserve some space of their own, later. In them may lie the great
hope of future falconry: domesticated breeds of hawks indepen-
dent of dwindling natural stocks, gyrs that will wait on, monster
merlins, hardier peregrines. But allow this romantic to hope
there will always be a place in the ancient sport for the wild hawk
caught on passage, one who had been hatched on an arctic cliff
instead of in a breeding chamber.

THE SECOND great group of birds used in historical falconry is
the accipiters or true hawks. Accipiters are a large,
worldwide group with more members than the falcons, but fewer
kinds are used in sport. Like the falcons, almost all accipiters are
built on the same plan, varying more in size and color than
in structure. They have round, staring eyes in wild primary
yellows and reds, set in small heads, shadowed by pronounced
ridges that to human observers give them a perpetually angry
look. They have long legs, long supple bodies, long, loose,
flexible tails, and feet like rat traps. Their wings are short and
rounded for maneuvering under the forest canopies where they
live; an accipiter cannot fly at sixty miles an hour, but it can turn

on a dime. Accipiters range in size from kestrel-sized true sparrow hawks to hulking three-pound goshawks. While the smallest birds—Europe's and Asia's sparrow hawks and America's sharpshins—are sometimes flown on quail and blackbirds, the larger members of the family are more useful. Our Cooper's hawk can take quail, rabbits, and the occasional pheasant. And the goshawk, bird of choice for the closed-country hawk enthusiast throughout the world, can take *anything*.

Gosses are found around the world through the boreal forest and its southward mountain extensions, with close relatives in Africa and Australia. They are a paradox. The "cuisinier" of the French, they are probably the most useful hawk in the world, the *only* hawk with any "practical" value. Some austringers in the northeast consistently take between ninety and a hundred head of game a year, mostly rabbit and some pheasants, an amount that could keep a family through the winter. But a goshawk is also among the most maddening animals on the planet, with a mind as alien to a human's as that of a thing from Alpha Centauri. They are aloof, brooding, schizoid predators, difficult to train, delicate and murderous, prone to strokes, fits, and lung disease. They are rarely affectionate. Their capacity for ignoring the falconer is unmatched. They fear strange people, dogs, cars, and phantoms. They tend to be grabby and vicious. Yet this bird that cringes from shadows while on the fist is used to hunt small deer in Pakistan (I have seen one *ride* a whitetail for fifty yards for no discernible reason) and will attack a man in defense of its nest. The accipiters' love of dense cover makes them invaluable in wooded country. They will get down on the ground and fight it out with a hare or pheasant like a gamecock, and follow rabbits into holes. And unlike the easygoing but lumbering hawks of the buteo group, they are fast enough to take a fair amount of winged game.

Goshawks, and for that matter all the rest of the hawks that we will consider, kill with the power of their talons rather than by the speed of an aerial strike. Getting hit on your bare hand by an enraged gos is just like sticking a fork into a light socket—a memorable experience, a blow to the gut. You need serious gloves, like a welder's, to handle a gos; no lightweight calf-leather numbers here. Although the death-from-above bomb burst of a peregrine may seem kinder, I doubt that a goshawk's victim feels much—the talons will penetrate its brain or heart in seconds. It is said that the talons of the hunting eagles of Kirghizstan penetrate to a wolf's vitals as swiftly.

Don't ask me why, but I love something about the gos. Despite the fact that they do not really love anything or anybody (captive breeding of accipiters is difficult because the females eat their mates in captivity like black widow spiders); despite the fact that I have nearly frozen to death waiting for one to come down; despite the fact that they will break your soft human heart by dying in twenty-four hours of aspergillosis or in ten seconds of a summer fit, they will always have a place in my mews. Some people are still flying goshawks they have had for eighteen years, nursing and coaxing them through all the inevitable troubles. And the old birds still stare out, uncaring, magnificent, viewing the whole world as a possible meal through lunatic blood red eyes.

Of the sharpshin there is little to tell. They combine accipiter personality and amphetamine energy in a five-ounce frame, and it is easier to kill them than to fly them. A few are caught by merlin trappers on the northeastern coast every year; almost all are released. A few masters, more patient and perhaps more masochistic than I, have flown them on sparrows and starlings with some success, but they are not for me, or for anyone but the kind of person who takes salmon on a two-ounce cane rod and shoots pigeons with a five-pound twenty-eight gauge shotgun.

The Cooper's hawk, of wide distribution mostly south of the

goshawk's range, is in every way intermediate between the sharpie and the gos. She is much sturdier than the sharpie, and even more tyrannical, hysterical, and demanding than the gos. Nevada's Harry McElroy, who has made a lifelong study of the Cooper's, advises wearing welding glasses when flying the hand-raised baby Coop that's lost her inhibitions about mankind.

Which brings up the second question most often asked about trained hawks: "Do they go for the eyes?" Mostly, no. A few overly tame accipiters *will* bounce off the highest annoying object—usually your head—and if they happen to grab an eye on the way, you will regret it. But very few hawks other than the gos will even defend their nests, never mind attack. It is worth remembering that, according to Konrad Lorenz, most predatory birds have an aversion to attacking eyes; it saves the nestlings from being blinded by their siblings before they fledge.

And incidentally, trivia buffs: it was a goshawk that took out Kirk Douglas's eye in *The Vikings*, and probably started the whole question in the first place.

THE BUTEO (buzzard) and eagle group contains all the other species of birds used in falconry. It is a less uniform collection than either the falcons or the accipiters, and in fact some of the birds in the group are probably as closely related to accipiters as they are to some of the other members of their own family. There are immense true eagles with feathers down to their toes and talons large as your hand; heavyset soaring hawks, hawk eagles like giant crested goshawks with feathered legs, and other oddities. But in very general terms, the group's members tend to be heavy and slow and more easygoing than either falcons or accipiters.

In historical falconry the only members of this group used were the golden eagle and a few of the accipiterlike hawk eagles.

During this century a few individuals, eccentric even among falconers, have tried out huge tropical eaters of monkeys and antelopes like the harpy and the crowned hawk eagles, usually with dire consequences for the neighborhood dogs.

America offers three members of this group found nowhere else; two of them are uniquely adaptable and one is more suited to specialists. The specialist's bird is the ferruginous hawk, found on the high plains from Canada to New Mexico. (Ferruginous simply means "rusty.") The "ferrug" of falconers—pronounded with a soft "g"—is the largest raptor on the continent except for the eagles, which it resembles. Some heretical biologists even consider it to be a hawk eagle, because of its feathered legs, size, and aggressiveness. It is a magnificent bird, found only in treeless country, where you can observe it sitting on the ground or soaring and tilting on the perpetual wind. It usually can be identified by the rusty "V" that its leg feathers make against its shining white underside. Although the ferrug used to be considered a close relative of the mouse-eating arctic rough-legged hawk, most ornithologists now believe it to be unique in both habits and structure. It generally refuses to sit in or fly around trees or to chase anything that is flying. It sports a large bill and an enormous mouth that cracks its head to 'way back beyond its eye, perhaps to facilitate its habit of swallowing large ground squirrels whole. Despite its bulk—up to six pounds in a big female—it is extremely agile on the wing, perhaps more so than its smaller relative, the redtail.

The ferrug's niche in falconry is as specialized as its niche in nature—it is considered the ultimate hawk for *large* jackrabbits. Some people consider it the only hawk that will consistently hold the biggest whitetailed jacks and European hares, which may weigh eight pounds and intimidate tiercel eagles. The ferrug prefers to make a start up to a quarter mile away from sitting quarry, and will often refuse close flushes. But once the big hawk is rolling, it is surprisingly speedy and very persistent. A few ferrugs have taken pheasant and even sage grouse, but they will only attempt sitting or running birds.

The redtail occupies a position in falconry analogous to that first old Chevy or maybe a battered but beloved twelve-gauge pump gun. And like these venerable workhorses, it is often sneered at by those who have moved on to Maseratis and hand-made English doubles. The 'tail deserves better than that. While unspectacular, the redtail is hardier, more reliable, and infinitely more agreeable than any accipiter. It is also smarter. "They got bigger heads—there's more room for brains," argues Ralph Buscemi. He had an old redtail that grew so tame he gave her the run of the neighborhood during the summer moult. It soon became obvious that she was killing pigeons from his half-wild flock, a feat that should have been impossible for such a slow-moving bird. Ralph devoted an afternoon to figuring out her method. He found that she would sit on the roof, watching the circling flock. When they attempted to land, she would lumber into the air and flush them. Then, wasting no time or energy, she would return to her perch. By evening the pigeons would be exhausted and Red would pick off her bird and carry it to the lawn where she would devour it amidst the suburban clutter of lawn chairs and tricycles and wading pool.

If I were allowed to have one bird back that I have owned, it would be a male redtail named Cinnamon. I hunted with him over seven years. It is not merely his efficiency I remember, but the whole complex bond, which included hunting, worries, and laughter and yes, some kind of friendship. During our years together, Cinnamon caught, in addition to many legitimate cottontails, snowshoe hares, and pheasants, assorted mice (usually in front of amused acquaintances), the frozen half-rabbit and feral cat mentioned before, and a plate of sliced turkey from the center of a Thanksgiving dinner table. He never learned that potato chips were not hawk food and would snatch them from any nearby hand. And despite all these petlike attitudes, he was a deadly hunting hawk. He once took seven rabbits in a day's hunting, the largest single day's bag I know of in New England. He might have taken more if he hadn't objected to my removing the last one from his talons, giving me a slam on the hand that ached for a week—the only time he ever "footed" me. He was stolen several years ago and I still miss him. If he hadn't been stolen I would almost certainly still have him. Unlike wide-ranging falcons or psychotic goshawks, redtails are almost never lost, and they are among the hardiest and longest-lived of all hawks. Heinz Meng, ornithologist and pioneer falcon breeder, had one old female for over thirty years—and she dined primarily on pigeon heads! Pigeons carry so many hawk diseases that until recently a more delicate hawk living on them was playing Russian roulette.

The redtail is a solid and handsome hawk, large and broad shouldered, with large dark eyes, heavy feet, and a noble profile. The characteristic orange rust tail comes in during the first moult and lends an unexpected bit of flash, like a brilliantly colored tie on a banker. In personality 'tails are almost stolid, though this in no way reflects on their performance in the field. Despite their flight, which is slow compared to a goshawk's, they take a wide range of prey species. In the wild they are ecological opportunists, unlike the superficially similar but duller and weaker common buzzard of Europe. To the rabbits and pheasants taken by Cinnamon, I could add to the list of redtail prey garter snakes, shrews, chipmunks, a chihuahua, a woodchuck, chickens, and two wild mallards—and this without going beyond reports by my immediate circle of acquaintances. One trained Florida bird I know of had an unsettling taste for diamondback rattlesnakes. You had to be sure her prey was dead before you approached.

Perhaps the unique American contribution to the falconer's

roster is the Harris (or Harris's) Hawk, *Parabuteo unicinctus*. As its name implies, it is not a true buzzard but an offshoot from the main stock, probably one that evolved in the New World tropics. In the United States it is native to the true cactus desert, where it breeds year-round and lives in loose family groups, dining on such diverse fare as woodpeckers, quail, pack rats, and rabbits. As its choice of prey would imply, the Harris is among the most versatile of hawks. It is as intelligent as the redtail and even friendlier, almost as swift as the goshawk, and—uniquely— hunts happily in doglike packs. Although their wild population is small, they breed in captivity like rabbits, producing two or even three broods a year. Because of this and because of the bird's amazing tolerance of humans, we can expect to see more and more of the Harris. Its only drawback as a falconer's bird is its sensitivity to cold; when the mercury drops to below 20° F, the usually willing Harris will huddle in a tree, refusing to fly. Except for this trait, the Harris is all things to all falconers. In fact, it makes falconry so effortless that some old-time hawkers with long experience in goshawks and longwings worry that it makes everything look *too* easy. Flying a Harris might give a beginner an unrealistic opinion of his own ability and allow him practices that would kill an accipiter or lose a falcon.

In appearance, the Harris Hawk takes some getting used to. With their vulturine profiles, gangling build, and long wader's legs, they don't look like falconer's birds at all. Their festive black and white and chestnut plumage, touched with clownlike yellow on their bare faces, is tropical and alien and downright *weird*. And it is hard to tell individuals apart, a trait that has led to the nickname "clone" for the species—outraging more reverent falconers, who fill the columns of *Hawk Chalk* with indignant letters.

The final bird of falconry found in America is the golden eagle. Although the bird has a long and honorable tradition in historical falconry—the Germans still prefer them for catching the huge European hare—very few Americans use them today. This is partially because of federal regulations—it is not impossible to get an eagle, only almost impossible—and partly because most falconers have more sense. The care of an eagle is a full-time occupation and only a few American falconers have had the time and devotion to spare—notably Idaho's Morlan Nelson and Wisconsin's Frances Hamerstrom, both of some fame even outside the falconry community. Eagles are both more intelligent and loyal and far more dangerous than any other birds of prey. Anything that can kill a wolf can maim a man. A female eagle may weigh thirteen pounds and be able to exert *hundreds* of pounds of pressure at the points of her talons. A zoo specimen with concrete-dulled claws once cracked a small bone in my hand through a too-light glove. And once you have been hurt by an eagle you are likely to flinch.

Eagles still excite my imagination. I have no desire to have one at the moment; you need unlimited time to train them and unlimited space to fly them. But I hope that a few diehard fanatics will keep this brand of hawking alive, chasing hares and foxes and coyotes in this most demanding branch of the sport.

2

A COBBLER BENDS over his work in a low-roofed turf hut at the edge of a coastal meadow near the village of Valkenswaard in Holland. As he pounds a nail into a sole a sudden chatter outside the hut's slit window catches his attention. A post standing directly in front of the window is topped by a miniature of his hut with a black-masked songbird tethered in front. This shrike is staring at a spot on the gray fall horizon and calling rhythmically. The cobbler looks in the same direction. His experienced eyes pick out a dot that he knows is a migrating peregrine moving quickly down the beach. He drops his tools and takes several strings into his hands, tugging at each to make sure that he knows which one works which lure. Now he is no longer a cobbler but a professional falcon trapper, born of a line that stretches back to the Middle Ages.

He pulls on the first string. It is attached at its other end to the top of a pole about twenty feet away, and has a white pigeon tethered to it about halfway along. When the string is slack the pigeon is able to hide in a box, but now he tugs the bird from its refuge to hang flapping in the air. All predators are opportunists. The pigeon's injured appearance and contrasting white color catch the peregrine's eye, and she turns toward the hut, flagged in like a bull to a matador's waving cape.

The shrike is shrieking in terror. It runs into its hut to hide.

The trapper lets go of the pigeon's string, and it too beats a retreat. He pulls his second string to reveal an old hooded falcon with a bundle of feathers attached to her feet. He hopes that the wild bird will believe she has a rival, a mannerless bird that has stolen her pigeon, and that she will come in even more certainly.

By now the wild falcon is circling. The trapper drops the "pole hawk's" string and pulls his third string, bringing still another white pigeon from its hut. He pulls until the pigeon is standing on an invisible circle on the turf.

The wild bird sees the pigeon appear and flies straight at it, made reckless by her jealousy of the pole hawk. She slams into the pigeon, grabs it, and breaks its neck, but when she tries to rise she finds that it is stuck to the ground. Mantling over it suspiciously, covering it with her wings, she begins to pluck its feathers, raising her head every few mouthfuls to glare at the unsuspecting placid pole hawk.

Then the cobbler pulls his final string, and pops a bow net over her head.

M OST FALCONERS' interest in birds goes back to a childhood memory so early and dim it seems inherited. I remember the terror and exhilaration of hawks chasing my father's racing pigeons, and I know I saw falcons in books and on television. But these glimpses did not make me a falconer. The obsession starts when you call a bird from the air. And the very first time you do that is more likely than not when you trust yourself to the unlikely lore of trapping. Trapping's implausibility is a good part of its charm. The birds are "up there," and it is hard for any novice to imagine that he can pull down a hawk from its native air by following a set of irrational sounding procedures passed down by word of mouth and (very sketchily) in print. It requires a certain suspension of disbelief even to picture the classic Valkenswaard setup for trapping passage falcons, used successfully from the Middle Ages to the First World War.

The naturalist Bil Gilbert has written about what he calls "getting-ready games," activities that you enter as necessary preliminaries to another sport, but which are fascinating enough to become ends in themselves. Fly-tying and stream entomology are getting-ready games that apply to fly-fishing. Decoy-making is a getting-ready game that was once attached to duck hunting but that has spawned a subculture and industry of its own, so there are decoy shows, scores of decoy books, and individual decoys that bring Mercedes Benz prices at auction. Falconry is a complicated game, and has spawned crafts, high-tech inventions, forms of subsidiary husbandry, and dependent sports. All these might qualify as getting-ready games. But hood-making, transmitter design, breeding, and pigeon derbies all pale in interest beside trapping, because trapping is itself a form of hunting. It is pure fun and suspense, a little like catch-and-release fly-fishing but with a quarry a lot fiercer than a trout and a little more like yourself.

Though the federal regulation forbidding the apprentice to take nestlings exists to ensure the survival of lost birds and to deter those unwilling to test their nerve, skills, and faith in the mysteries of trapping, it has the effect of practically guaranteeing the intelligent beginner a manageable bird. And there is an unforeseen result. As I might have predicted when I saw that first kestrel turn on the wind, trapping is nearly as addictive as falconry itself.

Some falconry books consciously avoid the subject of trapping on the grounds that any graphic account of how you catch a hawk would allow the "unqualified" to catch one. And many just skip over it entirely. The whole process of capturing hawks takes on a miraculous air, as if the hawk were magically transferred from the wild air to the falconer's glove. This reticence may stem from the fact that in our violent but sentimental age, practitioners of the so-called blood sports fear to admit that they must occasionally spill blood. While this is not a how-to book—I include no blueprints or knot-tying diagrams—it does purport to be a straightforward account. I'll no more apologize for the blood and guts than ignore the glory. And the plain ugly truth is that hawk-trapping uses and often kills pigeons.

Most falconers and virtually all longwingers keep pigeons. They are good, rich food for birds and for falconers, so rich that they are used more as a supplement than as a steady diet. They are essential in trapping. And for the same reason, they are the standard backup live lure. An encumbered and apparently handicapped pigeon is so irresistible that most hawkers carry a couple of live pigeons in their lure bags whenever they go afield. If a bird (remember that to a falconer a bird is a hawk, a pigeon only a pigeon) goes astray, the falconer will let out a doomed pigeon on a long string to call the bird back.

Perhaps a pigeon on a string looks so good because a pigeon flying free is more than a match for most hawks. Some competitive souls in the northern Rockies hold pigeon derbies where you bring your best hawk and best homer. You back your falcon against your competitors' pigeons, your pigeon against their hawks. In this case, the pigeon is more likely to win than even a peregrine. Still, I suspect that if pigeons had a mythology, falconers would be down there as some cross between Hitler and the devil. Or as a Maine falconer once put it to me after more than a couple of drinks: "If there's anything to reincarnation, I'd sure as shit hate to come back as a falconer's pigeon!"

The pigeon "rig" or "jacket" consists of a leather vest made to fit a pigeon, covered with monofilament nooses and dragging a weight or a ball of string. It is effective because it looks natural,

like a slightly handicapped pigeon. The jacket is the standard device for catching big longwings—peregrines, prairie falcons, and gyrfalcons—but it is versatile; most falconers who fly anything bigger than merlins use it at one time or another, and many simply keep a pigeon, a jacket, and some pigeon food in the car from September to January just in case they see something irresistible.

All hawks will show some interest. Tundra-bred peregrines are almost too easy, since you may well be the first person they have ever seen. They will sit on beaches during their migration and wait for you as you come up and throw them a pigeon. If you are careless and actually hit one, she may move at least three feet before she kills the pigeon. Redtails, who normally ignore birds, seem to sense the almost imperceptible handicap of the jacket and string; they rarely refuse a bait. And I know a trapper who had a merlin buzz his pigeon in the same spirit with which she would razz a hawk or raven. Unfortunately for her she snagged a trailing talon in a noose. My friend loves to display a photo that shows her crouched beside the monstrous homer with one foot extended and tethered to its back. Both birds look disgusted.

Finally this method is the best way to recapture lost birds. Even if they have reverted to the wild, they are likely to be unusually bold and unusually fond of pigeons. Often they will come in to kill any pigeon on a string and simply let you take them up. A couple of nooses can reassure the trapper.

You have to harden your heart when you use the jacket if you want it to work. If you run in immediately the hawk will try to get away, and her shock at being caught simultaneously by a human and a pigeon will cause her to ignore the bait bird entirely. But such hawks are usually caught by only one noose—insufficient to hold anything bigger than a merlin—and even a hawk can put two and two together sufficiently well to get suspicious of the next couple of gift-wrapped pigeons. It is safer for all but the bait to let her kill and pluck and partially eat it, by which time she'll be stuck like a fly in flypaper.

Details in such things as traps are vitally important, and very small changes in design can make the difference between a bird in the hand and frustration. A couple of years ago I got a message that a friend's lost prairie-peregrine hybrid was alive and well and killing pigeons in the vicinity of the USS *Constitution* Museum on Boston Harbor. She had flown away twenty miles west of Boston three weeks earlier, so I was sure that when I got to the harbor I'd see a kestrel or more likely nothing at all. But as I entered the narrow waterfront street from the elevated expressway, a flock of pigeons exploded from beneath the bridge, followed by a dark silhouette bigger and much faster than any gull. I screeched to a stop in front of the museum, grabbed a jacketed pigeon, and jumped out.

The birds had disappeared. Now, I am a self-conscious person, and not given to waving birds around on public streets at two o'clock in the afternoon. I have a little of the falconer's paranoia about showing my birds to an unenlightened public, and a little of the prudent sportsman's more sensible aversion to shedding blood in front of people who think that meat is manufactured in the supermarket. If you pile these inhibitions on top of each other you will realize how much I wanted that bird. It was a desire less connected to helping my friend than to a visceral hawk-possession lust. Because my next act was to plant my feet on that sidewalk and wave that unlucky pigeon like a flag.

Nothing.

Again. Yelling, "HOO! HO! HO! HO! HAWK!"

And she circled back into view over the expressway bridge, two hundred feet overhead, setting her wings for a second and looking back over her shoulder.

And I threw the pigeon as high as I could, yelling "HO!" She turned over on her back and came down on it like a hammer. It exploded and fell bleeding and stone dead onto the museum's tiny lawn. She climbed, turned, and ripped past again, rolling the pigeon ten feet along the ground, climbed, turned, and buzzed by three feet from my face, shrieking defiance. It was obvious that I wasn't going to pick her up easily.

I think there were at least ten horrified spectators standing by, but to this day I don't remember their faces. All my attention was on the hawk. Beside the museum was an abandoned pier with a surface of pavement and sand. I scooped up the pigeon, not an easy job since the falcon's blow had cleaved it nearly in half, ran out onto the pier, and tossed it on the ground.

The falcon was coursing in circles, yelling. I raised my gloved hand in some kind of ludicrous attempt to call her in and she tagged it hard enough to numb my knuckles, then veered away still screaming. After she made two more hits on my gloved hand I retreated about fifty yards from the pigeon. She strafed it with one last pendulum strike, then landed on it as lightly as a butterfly. After glaring around for a moment she began to pluck it.

As I watched it became obvious that the nooses had all been attached to the back of the jacket and were now under the pigeon's body as she fed on the breast. I hadn't noticed the defect until that moment. No amount of reading can convey to you the sense of such practical details as where to place nooses, or the little unnatural rock backward you give the "bird hand" as you place the hood on a hawk's head. Only experience or another falconer can teach you.

I decided to try to pick her up anyway. When she had nearly finished I took a firm grip on a hunk of chicken giblet with my gloved hand and began to crawl across the pier. My concentration was focused on the bird, who now began to mantle and cluck ominously. I flattened out and wriggled on my belly, muttering "Good girl, *good* girl, c'mon, here's your dinner." She wasn't having any of it. When I was about three feet from her, with her looming above me like a mountain, she leaped, grabbed the giblet, bounced, smacked me on the forehead, and took off. Now her shrieks sounded triumphant. As I dusted off my knees she disappeared around a warehouse. I was to see her once more, three days later, sharing the roof of that same warehouse with one of the winter's transient snowy owls. But it was to be another month before a luckier or more skillful friend picked her up. I know for a fact his pigeon had nooses on its breast as well as its back since we had discussed the problem after my failure.

As a postscript to this minor adventure and as a portrait of a true falcon fanatic, I might add that when I called the bird's owner that evening I asked why he hadn't told me how aggressive the bird was.

"Aggressive? She's not aggressive!" He paused for a moment. "Of course, once last year she did knock my daughter flat on her back in the field, but she was just *playing*."

T HE SWEDISH GOSHAWK trap is another trap that uses pigeons, though it doesn't kill them. Its name sounds ludicrous, like "yellow-bellied sapsucker," but it may be the most effective hawk-catching machine in existence. It resembles an A-frame house on stilts, with doors as the upright sides of the "A." A box of pigeons lives beneath the floor; a perch hinged in the middle holds the doors open until the curious hawk sits on it, at which point they clap shut with a bang. A goshawk trap works because you leave it in the woods, far from human interference, and only visit it once a day. A suspicious hawk can study the trap for an hour if she chooses. Because you do not remove the hawk immediately you build the trap large—the one I used to use had a floor about three by four—and stretch soft, yielding netting rather than chicken wire on the sides.

I set my first goshawk trap on somebody else's land with the connivance of a local poacher and backwoodsman, for the simple reason that we saw more hawks there. The mild illicit flavor of the project made it that much more fun. Though fun wasn't exactly the word for carrying a cumbersome box half a mile into the woods at three in the morning. It was raining, the land was hilly, and at one point we had to balance our way across a defunct beaver dam. Deer kept stumbling up in the glow of Dave's miner's lamp, giving us what I figured were looks of disbelief. But we got the trap in place before dawn.

Then the fun began. I would sneak in every afternoon just before dusk with a rise of anticipation so fierce and pure it felt like sickness, like apprehension, like fear. The fact that I had to sneak in, avoiding driveways and paths, made the daily journey even more intense. Approaching the trap I would circle, always afraid that, though it was a remote part of the estate, someone would have found and destroyed the trap, or, worse, would be waiting.

Added to all this was the grab-bag nature of the Swedish trap. It might catch anything—a goshawk (and if it did, would it be a legal first-year adult or an old haggard?) a redtail, a Cooper's hawk, great horned or barred owls, even a raccoon capable of destroying the pigeons and the rig. As the trap became visible through the trees I would freeze and squint at it, trying to resolve a hawk from the mosaic of shadows and lines. I knew that if there was a gos she would probably be active, leaping straight up and banging her brainless red-eyed head against the roof, hanging by her talons on the sides like a deranged monkey. But if the trap had collected an owl, he would most likely just sit and blink until you were about a foot from the trap.

This particular trap caught three hawks: a haggard male gos, a haggard male redtail and, amazingly, a six-ounce passage sharpshin. We released the redtail with some difficulty; he refused to leave, even when the trap was opened, but sat back on his tail in an intimidating posture of fear, crest up, pupils dilating and contracting, bill open. I finally took him and tossed him straight up, where he recovered from his paralysis in midair and flapped heavily off. The gos was a little harder for us to throw away. After all, he was the right species, but laws aside, he was old, with a silver breast and dark red eyes, a certain sire of more local goshawks and as spooky and set in his ways as a leopard. When we opened the doors he didn't hesitate but rowed away so fast that it was impossible to believe he had been there at all.

The sharpie was another case. When we approached we could hear her mad fluttering before we could even see the trap. She was whipping around in the box in a kind of insectile fury like a predatory butterfly and for a moment I doubted the wisdom of so much as touching her for fear she would explode or die. I did not particularly want her as a falconer's bird, but I had a friend who was banding migratory hawks, and though I was a little afraid of her delicacy I could hardly resist holding so much fury. I pushed my jacket through the crack in the doors and dropped it over her so that I could slow her down long enough to pinion her wings.

She was wholly alien, superficially like a tiny goshawk but with long toothpick legs, two-inch bird-grabbing toes tipped in thin recurved daggers, and impossibly huge and artificial dayglo yellow eyes. What she was doing trying to catch pigeons that outweighed her three to one, how hard she had to hit the trigger to collapse the doors, I'll never know. Though I knew she was impossibly delicate and wild I had a moment's rush of that lust to possess that inflames anybody when they hold something perfect.

I slipped her into a child's sock with a hole cut in the toe so that her head protruded from the hole. It had a leather thong laced around it to make sure it didn't slip down over her bottle shoulders. Later the sock could be cut off, but meanwhile I could carry her in my hand or my pocket without damaging her feathers.

From some combination of October sunshine, late-afternoon laziness, and triumph we decided to walk the footpath. We were strolling along, the sharpie swinging in my hand like a rolled newspaper, when we heard the thud of running footsteps. We froze for a moment, thinking we'd run; then I laid the hawk flat behind the stone wall beside the track and sat on the wall, folding my arms and attempting to look casual. A moment later a very fat jogger dressed in a tomato red running suit to match his face rounded the corner. He continued to jog up to us and we nodded a greeting. He more or less stopped and, jogging in place, wheezed: "You *do* know this is private property?"

"Just watching the birds." He nodded cordially enough, wiped his face with a white handkerchief, and began to jog slowly forward again. When he rounded the corner we held our breath for a moment more, then began laughing hysterically. It was five minutes before I regained enough wind to bend over the wall and pick up the bird.

H OWEVER PLEASANT the Christmas-morning surprises of attending an unmanned woods trap, I still prefer trapping migrants "mano a mano." The suspense is even more unbearable, the skills needed harder to perfect, and the prize comes to *you*. This kind of trapping is so exciting that it is by no means confined to falconers. Maybe some hawk banders are so solemn that they believe that they can trap hawks only for pure scientific knowledge. But most are honest enough to admit that the lore, the fascination, the adrenalin, are all addictive, that they trap for pleasure every bit as much as the falconer does.

In October on the coast of New England merlins fill the air and trees after the passing of every storm front. At this time of year a pond or marsh in the coast country will look like a textbook diagram of predation, with warblers and flycatchers chasing insects in the surface film, hyperactive pickerel slashing up from below, merlins and sharp-shinned hawks following the songbirds as if they were attached to them by short strings. When the weather is right you may see ten raptores in as many minutes. But the trouble with trying to trap these merlins is that because of their aerial skill they are usually stuffed full of songbird half an hour after they wake up. Through field glasses their crops can be seen to bulge as if they had just swallowed oranges, and there is little incentive for them to come to your baits.

So according to friends who live in merlin country, you must take advantage of some other habits of these small hawks. First, these enterprising trappers would kill a pigeon that weighed three times as much as a merlin and strew its downy feathers around a yard or two of ground. Then the trappers added the touch that lifted their plans from mundanity to genius. Most small hawks will chase other birds of prey (and ravens and gulls and terns) seemingly for the sheer energetic hell of it. And if the pursued bird drops something that the little pirate can use, so much the better. So my friends would tether a hapless tame kestrel beside the pigeon carcass, and wait.

It's hard to avoid a little anthropomorphism at this point. Here comes a merlin that has just flown in from Newfoundland. She sees this grasshopper hawk holding a hawk's equivalent of a whole cow, thinks: "All I have to do is buzz the little wimp once at fifty miles an hour and it's *all mine*." And she does. But crafty humans have hung a nearly invisible collapsing net—a "dho ghazza" in falconry Pakistani—right behind the kestrel, and the next moment she's balled like a fly in a spider's web, cursing her

captors in a screech that seems to be just on the painful edge of human hearing.

The elegance and necessary complication of the plan made it at least as irresistible to me as to any merlin. When I watched a five-ounce male taken by this method fly from a field where a friend was schooling him into a dumpster in a busy parking lot to kill a sparrow, I was impressed. I wanted one of those right now! I could hardly wait for the trapping permits, and I was more than ready when the call came at last.

Our first task was formidable. We had to pack a monstrous load of tackle and live bait across a half mile of unfamiliar mud flats, thickets, and tidal creeks to the trapping site. This had to be done before full light; even a merlin's boldness has its limits. We deployed our traps at the edge of the sand and retreated beneath yards of camouflage netting to wrap ourselves in blankets and drink coffee and wait. And wait. And wait. The day dawned shrouded with fog, clammy and bone chilling. The only sound was the lapping of water on the rocks behind us and the intermittent thrumming of a lobster boat's engine somewhere in the mist. Nothing was visible out to sea but fog, nothing to landward but a black dripping line of spruce.

The essence of sitting in blinds is boredom, cold, and the question, "What the hell am I doing here?" Boredom above all—we overcivilized creatures are not used to waiting and watching and doing nothing. But if you wait, shiver, and are bored long enough, you will see things. Three hours after we settled in, the kestrel bobbed his head and stared intently at a spot on the tree line. Binoculars spun into focus revealed a sharp-shinned hawk with the mad yellow eyes of a first-year bird, hunched down in the foliage of a spruce. It seemed to stare right down the barrels of my field glasses into my head. For a moment the bird held its pose, regarding me as if I were some kind of enormous prey. Then it dropped from the tree, leveled out three

feet above the ground and disappeared into the mist with the characteristic three-beats-and-a-glide flight of the accipiters. It obviously didn't care for our baits.

For four more hours we froze without seeing any sign of life other than our bait. I imagined he looked bored. A soft breeze from somewhere made us even colder but blew holes in the mist so that we could see the piles of boulders appearing and disap-

pearing to seaward. I was watching the play of fog and water drowsily, as you watch a fire or an aquarium, when I was brought back to the present by a shriek from the kestrel. I turned to see a raven land beside him on the rock and stop, staring. The kestrel bounced and chittered, but the raven just continued to stare, motionless. I stood up and yelled. When the raven still hesitated I flung a hunk of driftwood at him. He floated into the air and curved away downwind, croaking his disappointment. I felt bad for both birds. Right now all we were doing was annoying the locals, and from the continuing chatter of the kestrel I was sure that the little cow-pasture bug hawk had never dreamed of crows that large.

No other raptores passed that day, only a flock of crows and a lonely cormorant. At dusk we dismantled the traps and stumbled out on legs made stiff by hours of too little movement. As we ate supper on the tailgate in the day's last glow I saw a sharp-winged figure flying over the edge of the trees. I pointed wildly trying to force an exclamation through a mouthful of hot dog. My friend saw it first. "Peregrine!" he whooped. The bird circled once, an enigmatic falcon-shaped silhouette, and vanished. I wasn't sure, but peregrine or merlin, it seemed like a good omen for the next day.

The next day, though, was more of the same. It was just as foggy, just as wet and cold. The kestrel picked disconsolately at his cold pigeon breast. We were all twice as stiff, and no birds flew in the morning at all. By noontime I was bumming cigarettes despite a promise to myself not to smoke, and feeling more than a little restless. However much I might believe in the ideal of sitting bored in blinds as a path to enlightenment, the practice was making me crazy. By the end of the evening I was drinking Scotch straight up in a beer mug. We didn't go to sleep until three, and our five o'clock rising was a predictably soggy one.

The weather was worse, but hangover and cold had brought me to that state where you accept either failure or success with equanimity. I could enjoy the sights. At nine o'clock the kestrel spotted a merlin on a spruce at the edge of the cove to the south. We crouched, barely daring to breathe, covering our shining faces. I wiggled myself into a position where I could see out through my binoculars. She was clearly interested in our circus, staring at the baits and bobbing her head. But as she started to fly a shadow passed over us. I looked up to see an immature bald eagle stroking across the sky no more than twenty feet above our heads. The great bird was seven feet across, streaked brown and dirty white, with a huge bill like a cigar. The merlin dropped from her perch with loud shrieks of delight and chased the eagle out of sight around the point, circling the bigger bird as it flew. Her voice echoed back a moment longer before the fog swallowed it up. Soon afterward the mist blew away, transfiguring the dull grass and spruce, turning them to gold and deep rich green. Behind us were islands stretching pale in the sun as far as we could see. We had trapping weather at last. But the merlins were gone, vanished to the south, and it was time to go home.

SOME CONTEMPORARY TRAPPING techniques are as ludicrously simple as Valkenswaard's three-ring circus was complicated. The final refinement, the ultimate no-tech rig, and the most intimate form of all trapping is the dig-in. While there are rumors that American Indians caught golden eagles and condors by

hiding in baited pits, the modern dig-in seems to be an invention of the peregrine trappers of the 1940s and 1950s in such places as the Outer Banks and the Gulf Coast of Texas. You drive your jeep along the ocean side of the barrier beach until you see a tundra peregrine sitting on the ground. While the driver sits idling and watching the bird, you jump out on the opposite side, dig a shallow pit, crawl in, and cover your legs with sand and your head and shoulders with a sort of wastebasket woven of wire and beach grass. Your hands are left free and in them you hold a boldly patterned live pigeon. Your friend drives away. The pigeon flaps. *Falco peregrinus tundrius* flies over and kills the pigeon while you maintain a firm hold on its legs. When the hawk begins to eat, you transfer your grip to her legs, throw off the wastebasket with your free hand, and holler for your friend.

It was just that simple if you knew the habits of peregrines, and that effective. During the first years, incredible as it might seem now when Arab princes pay premium prices for peregrines and breeders squander fortunes to produce them, the trappers would *release* five "blond birds"—their name for the then scientifically unrecognized pale-crowned *tundrius* subspecies—in order to get one dark-headed *anatum* or "duck hawk." They had observed that come spring the tundra birds would develop wanderlust and, if not immediately retired to the molt for the summer, would set out for the arctic.

After DDT virtually eliminated the *anatum*, diehard peregrine aficionados, the hardest core of the hard core of falconry, continued to trap tundra birds until all peregrines came under federal protection in 1970. Though it is a more than delicate subject among falconers, laws rarely put an end to activities passionately engaged in by people who think they are right. For several years after the closing of the beaches a bunch of peregrine fanatics continued to seek the grail, evading the shore patrols with the same gusto they brought to hawking. Though I am no apologist for poachers, it is hard to fault the bandits on ecological or aesthetic grounds. Although often portrayed by federal wardens, who should know better, as a bunch of profiteers supplying some dark market, they were in fact a bunch of informed if lawless hedonists who flew their own prizes for one season and then let them go. Considering that as much as 80 percent of hawk mortality takes place in the first year among birds learning to hunt, you could argue that by giving their birds both a guaranteed meal ticket and plenty of hunting experience the bandits ensured their winter survival and gave them a good shot at returning to the ancestral breeding grounds. No less an authority than Cornell's Tom Cade argued for years for a similar licensed program on the grounds that it would bolster the wobbling arctic population.

These survivals from a more carefree age flew birds ten days off the beach, flew at doves in East Coast pastures and cheered their birds when they left to complete their migration. They brought a lightheartedness to the sport that I confess I miss in these days of electronics and captive breeding. I remember one grizzled veteran who unhooded his blond *tundrius* as his dog vibrated on point in a cornfield during the second week of October.

"Uhh . . . if you don't mind my asking . . . how long have you had her?"

"Two weeks."

"And how long have you been flying her loose?"

"Son, you're gonna *see* it. This is her first flight."

She killed her pheasant dead in the air, then shared the kill with the old falconer as if she had been doing so all her life. I heard later that she killed quite a few more pheasants before she headed north in April. I still find it hard to see what harm her temporary custodian inflicted on her or on her species.

For better or for worse, his kind are gone. With the federalizing and bureaucratization of falconry we have gained nominal if not always effective protection of our birds and a ban on the hideous persistent pesticides, even if we have lost some of our anarchic freedom. But some good stories still come down from those times. A couple of years back I had a tentative agreement from *Rolling Stone* magazine to do an interview with Chris Boyce, the "falcon" half of the infamous falcon and snowman espionage team. Before the project fell apart Boyce and I had many long phone conversations, mostly about falconry. He told me of innocent if already illegal days spent trapping on the Texas coast. He used to disguise himself as a surf fisherman and on one occasion begged assistance from a federal warden to pull out his mired dune buggy. As they talked of tides and fish, Boyce was acutely aware that under the seat lay a trussed, newly trapped *tundrius*.

This story may say something sad about adrenalin addiction and bored youth. I don't know. But I do hope that, as peregrines repopulate the states, beach trapping will be opened again. Can you imagine the feeling in your heart when a bird turns those eyes on you and darts to your hands like an arrow? For just one moment you must be both the predator and the prey.

3

"...the Eyas Hawke, upon whom I can fasten no affection..."
—Edmund Bert, 1619

I N SPRING a falconer's fancy turns to thoughts of eyases. Trapping is still the most exciting way to get a bird. But these days probably 75 percent of the birds flown by falconers begin their domestic careers as babies, either from a wild nest or from a breeding chamber.

Through most of hawking's history the percentages were reversed. Although eyases are *de facto* tamer than passagers, I suspect that their infantile-cum-Godzilla behavior has driven more beginners away from falconry than any other single factor. Bert's remarks in 1619 about the stupidity and unfocused ferocity of nestlings are still valid today. He complained that the average eyas "would hang with their head downward, holding a bough fast with her foote or feete." (The grammar is pure Bert.) He adds: "I have known some of them likewise that would sooner catch a dogge in the field than a Partridge, and although she had flown a Partridge well to marke, and sat well, yet so soon as a dog had but come in to the retrove, she would have had him by the face."

What's more, eyases—at least those that I'd call accidental

imprints*—scream. And scream. And scream. And scream. And scream. Imagine ten pages, or fifty, covered with this phrase. Turn it up so that your ears ring. Is your bird a redtail? Make it hoarse. Start it at five A.M. Feed it and listen to the interesting modulations that screaming while swallowing makes. Scream! Scream! Scream! Scream! Screa(gleep)m! Scream!

Two months later (scream! scream! scream!) you are also having aggression problems. Your bird "mantles"—braces herself like an animated umbrella over her food. (scream! scream! scream!) When you try to pick her up she foots your hand. (scream! scream! scream!) *Nobody* is strong enough to pull a redtail's talons out of a glove (scream!) so you wait. (Scream!—I assume the hawk is locked on the glove rather than on your bare hand—scream!) After a half hour of the hawk's demented, pupil-contracted, open-mouthed, raised-crested stare, she relaxes and begins to eat. She may even stop yelling for a minute, until she finishes eating. Then it all begins again.

You take her out to hunt. She tries to fly after a rabbit, but she is so excited and aggressive that she forgets to let go of the glove. (Scream!) She flops over upside down, comes up in a fury with crest raised to attack the enemy glove.

In the following February her screaming lets up. And she falls in love with you. While not entirely losing her aggression, she begins to direct it outward. She attacks your mate.

Years ago, when I lived in an apartment, I kept, in addition to a goshawk for real hunting, an imprint kestrel that I had rescued from a shoe box under the bed of a twelve-year-old would-be falconer. A falconer's parakeet, she was allowed free-flight privileges except in the hawk mews where the goshawk would have

---

*"Imprinting" is an ethological term adopted by falconers. An imprinted bird believes that you are its parents, and so directs its infantile begging (and later, often, its sexual impulses) to you.

considered her a delicacy, and in the living room. I had banished her from the living room at the request of friends because of her slashing attacks on their heads. If she was accidentally knocked down by their frantic gestures of self-defense ("Do they go for the eyes?") she would rush at their feet like a psychotic feathered chihuahua.

I never took any of this seriously—in fact, I'm sorry to admit, I thought it was funny. I even managed to be amused at her peculiar habit of stuffing the half-eaten carcasses of lab mice into my shoes for storage. Until one morning I woke to feel something tearing my forehead off. I yelled and sat up flailing wildly at what resolved itself into my eight-ounce falcon in that hysterical tantrum that was so amusing when directed at somebody else. I ducked out at a dead run, trying to shield all of my naked body at once, and slammed the door. In the bathroom mirror my face was not pretty. My forehead, cheek, and upper eyelid looked as if they had been tattooed with an icepick. After she calmed down I searched the room trying to find what had triggered the attack and found half of a dead chick under my pillow.

So why do so many contemporary falconers bother with such monsters? Part of the reason, sadly, is bureaucratic. Constantly catching and releasing hawks, while legal, generates massive paperwork and tends to make governmental monitors suspicious. But there are also positive reasons to fly an eyas. Even Bert admitted that if you could persevere through your baby's prolonged infancy you would have a superior hawk. Eyases are fearless and almost impossible to lose. Since they don't know what constitutes normal hawk fare, they will fly well against huge or unpalatable prey, should that be your desire. And they *like* you.

"The hand-raised eyas . . . flies to you because she loves you, not because she's hungry," wrote Kent Carnie in appreciation of his first captive-bred eyas. Passage birds still offer incomparable dash and polish in the air. But for the average falconer, a little slowness to learn or a bit of "talking" seems a small price to pay for a good eyas's fidelity and friendliness, especially now that the modern understanding of development and imprinting exemplified in Ronald Stevens's *Observations on Modern Falconry* and Harry McElroy's *Desert Hawking* allows you to eliminate the worst screaming and aggression.

W HAT IS this bird doing?" We were sitting in the kitchen of a pioneer falcon breeder, eleven years ago, after a day in the field. I stared at the photo in confusion. What I saw was a snapshot of my host grinning out at me from beneath what resembled a Maine lobsterman's sou'wester. An inflated innertube encircled his brow like a halo, while an obviously excited prairie tiercel balanced atop it all, flapping to keep his balance.

Was my new friend testing me? Was it some kind of "in" joke? Although Les was a serious and quiet man, he seemed to be suppressing a burst of laughter.

"What could it be doing? Is it attacking?" I muttered, knowing that it couldn't be anything so simple.

"Well, let me give you a hint." He passed me a second photo, one with a pair of falcons copulating. I looked from one to the other and at least a piece of the puzzle fell into place. The tiercel was making passionate love to the hat. But *why?*

Today anyone in falconry knows the answer to that question. In fact, in the 1981 issue of the *Journal of the North American Falconers Association*, different styles of "semen collection hats" are described and illustrated by Lester Boyd and Charles Schwartz. "We use a two-inch-diameter neoprene tube attached to the hat, with silicon caulking to form a gutter to catch the semen. Neoprene tubing is popularly used to pad roll bars on trucks and handlebars on dirt bikes. . . . In order to prevent the semen from soaking into the hat material, it can be waterproofed by rubbing it with paraffin."

Breeding is changing from an obsessive goal pursued by a few backyard visionaries into a conservation tool, a business, and maybe even into man's latest domestication. It is a miracle that is becoming so commonplace that special state and federal legislation is in the making to deal with such matters as domestic hawks and unprecedented hybrids. As long as the only source of birds was the wild, falconers' birds were legitimately considered wildlife; their "owner" was the state, rather than the individual, and laws minutely specified who could keep what and how. But with breeders producing second- and third-generation captive-bred birds, the whole question of ownership begins to take on complex legal and moral overtones. Is the captive-bred hawk a domestic animal? And if so, does the state have any legitimate control over its breeding, or even its sale? Recently, federal law has been amended to permit sales of most captive-bred raptores. To date not all states have followed suit.

Some breeding establishments, like the one at Cornell that is responsible for the reintroduction of the endangered peregrine into the wild, are immense bird factories backed by money from both institutional and private donors. Others are simple backyard flight pens with a pair or two of birds. These private projects cost a lot of money and time. To produce birds you need as an absolute minimum an incubator, a sturdy and inevitably expensive structure to house the breeders, and a lot of quality foodstuff like Coturnix quail. Not to mention the patience to either leave a natural pair of birds strictly alone, neither flying them at game nor even letting them see you for a couple of *years*, or else to train the males to copulate with your hat and the females to accept artificial insemination.

Breeders are serious people, though. They think more in terms of producing new hunting birds and increasing the scientific knowledge of falcon taxonomy than of just how funny it is to haunt four-wheeler shops looking for tubing to use in perverse activities with hawks. Their almost intimidating single-mindedness has brought them to the point where they can produce any given species or cross of falcon as certainly as a Kentucky farm can turn out a thoroughbred colt.

They have also shown that all large (and perhaps most small) falcons can produce fertile hybrids as easily as breeds of dogs can produce fertile hybrids. There are now in existence healthy and aggressive crosses of such unlikely species as merlins and gyrfalcons, three-way peregrine *x* prairie *x* merlin, and such oddities (more interesting to scientists than to field hunters) as kestrel *x* peregrines and bat falcon *x* peregrine. Such malleability unnerves a few conservationists, who fear that exotics like lanners or artificial hybrids might escape and endanger struggling native peregrine populations. The best argument against such worries is that it hasn't happened yet. Although many of the large falcon species live side by side—peregrines and prairies in America, peregrines and lanners and sakers and migrant gyrs in Eurasia— there has *never* been a recorded instance of hybridization in the wild, even in Western Europe where virtually all large species have been imported and lost over the centuries. Falcons are apparently "reproductively isolated" by behavior: they have different courtship rituals, nesting habits, prey preferences, and timing. A breeder can break down these barriers by artificial insemination or by isolating a bird with a potential mate of another species, but it is always a struggle.

The results can be spectacular. The most interesting high-plains grouse hawks today are gyr-peregrines that have all the gyr's size and speed but add a bit of the peregrine's docility and stooping ability. And gyr-merlins, like merlins but large enough to take pigeons and quail, may be among the most exciting new longwings for those of us who can't take off four months to go hawking. To be fair, some of the hybrids are not quite so prepossessing. In addition to some of purely academic interest, I have handled a gyr-prairie tiercel that combined the hysterical mood swings of the gyr with the inherent stubbornness of a prairie. Despite his speed, I passed on flying him.

It is hard to think of these birds as purely wild animals. And it seems to be simple justice to allow their breeders, who have stayed in the game for knowledge and the simple love of hawks, to recoup a little of the cost of their dedication. Their financial future remains clouded; still, I am sure they will find the support to continue, one way or another. I remember the enthusiasm in one master breeder's voice as he rambled on about "making" new birds. Some, more paranoid than I, might hear an echo of Frankenstein's monster. But to me it sounds like the beginnings of a new domestication, where down-home Yankee ingenuity combines ancient art with modern science to produce another partner for man.

THE TRADITIONAL way to get a baby hawk is to rob a nest. I have a friend who is a southerner, a vegetarian, and a drawling deadpan wit. Unlike many vegetarians he doesn't disapprove of hunting, but he used to get an unholy joy out of embarrassing me at urban social gatherings with references to my atavistic passions. He had code words for my pastimes—flyfishing was torturing fish with chicken feathers, hunting was killing innocent little animals. But somehow he could make falconry sound worse than either. "I'd like you to meet my friend Steve. He robs birds' nests, takes the babies, and makes killers out of 'em."

It wasn't the "killers" part. Even the most trendy nouveau-eco Jacques Cousteau baby-seal defender usually realizes that predators are predators. It's the "robs nests" that seemed to reach down deep into the souls of civilized folk and give me the status of a child molester. Perhaps it was a vestige of the childhood belief, strong at least in the fifties suburbs where I grew up, that mother birds can somehow smell any interference with their nests and will then desert them—a belief entirely without basis in fact. (Though it persists; the six-year-old son of a friend showed me a bucket of eggs he was soaking for twenty-four hours in salt water to remove the smell before he "gave them back"; I advised hard boiling as kinder.) And maybe a few more sophisticated bird enthusiasts are turned off by the excesses of such well-publicized hawk bandits as those who keep attempting to raid the Morro Rock peregrine eyrie.

But in fact, restrained nest-robbing is good for the population of the plundered species. First, the falconer immediately liberates the nestling that he takes from the vagaries of weather and food supply. Less obviously, when you take one or two young from a nest containing three or more birds you are increasing the chances that the remaining young will get enough food to grow to maturity. In many birds of prey that hatch several young, the smaller babies will die of starvation long before they fledge unless their larger competition is removed. And lest you think this is some sophistical falconer's version of the deer hunter's cliché "I'm killing them for their own good," let me remind you that unlike the deer the falconer's bird may return to the wild and breed. Whereas in a population at saturation levels there is no place for a surplus, in a threatened species like the peregrine or in one like the goshawk that is continually shifting and re-occupying second-growth woodlands the "surplus" birds become an obvious reservoir of new breeders.

As for the imagined pain of bereavement of the parents, it seems not to exist. Birds cannot count. As long as at least one youngster remains in the nest, the parents will return as soon as the falconer departs. (Goshawks never leave—they're too busy bouncing off the robber's head.) If *all* the young are taken the parents are unable to repeat the behavior cycle coded into their heads and may not return next year. "Raking" an eyrie is therefore rightly considered a heinous crime. Falconers value eyries as if they were the mother lode, hoarding them, trading them, and protecting them. I know a New England goshawker who fells trees across trails a good mile from his nests lest trail bikers disturb the birds.

What may not show through all this moral scientific data is that robbing nests, like trapping, is a getting-ready game that is just pure fun. After my abortive childhood beginning with kestrels I progressed to the New England falconer's bird of all work, the goshawk. To find them was a worthy challenge. According to conventional wisdom goshawks are rare birds outside the boreal forest. Probably even as recently as twenty-five years ago they were, not because temperate forests are in any way unsuited for gosses but because until recently the forest in such places as southern New England was not mature enough to attract them. As the trees that had reclaimed the old farms stretched past thirty feet, the old inhabitants began to trickle back. Porcupines and fishers began to edge in closer to the housing developments, and the shadowy Eastern coyote, perhaps the "wolf" of the colonists, howled again around the hill farms. By the time humans noticed these more spectacular forest dwellers the gos was already as common in the woods as the redtail was in the farmlands or the kestrel in the suburbs.

Which did not mean that they were easy to find. The gos requires a large woodlot to produce enough food for its voracious young. Unlike the soaring redtail it stays under the canopy, moving swiftly through places where the visibility is at best a couple of hundred feet. Since the gos defends its nest, a few hikers and trail bikers and riders find goshawks every year by the simple expedient of getting hit on the head. Whether they are as pleased as falconers to see a red-eyed bird with a four-foot wingspan accelerating at them screaming "Kukukukuk!" is debatable.

Falconers attempt to be a little more scientific. The first place to look is near previously used nest sites. Goshawks will not necessarily reuse a nest but they will build their new nests close to the old ones. A woodland niche will be continually occupied unless and until it is cut down and turned into a condo development. If one bird of a pair dies, its partner will stay. Soon a new mate will appear from the pool of younger wandering birds. I know goshawk nest sites that have produced young every year for fifteen years.

If you have no old sites to check, the procedure is slower but still pretty rational. During the winter you study topographical maps for the right combination of slope, exposure, and isolation. Like most raptores goshawks like to bathe daily, so you look for a little water—a small stream will do. Local knowledge becomes important. In the more southerly portions of their range goshawks choose the forks of hardwood trees; from Maine north they seem to prefer to locate their nests in big conifers close to the trunk.

Sooner or later you will take your data to the woods. If you start your search before the trees leaf out you can see nests, but the hawks will not defend their territory. You have to be content with more subtle clues, with old nests and glimpses of gray feather. You walk, stop, listen, and go on, then stop again. Was that a hawk, or a pileated woodpecker? If you are lucky you may find a plucking post, a stump or rock strewn with squirrel fur and grouse feather where the birds clean and dismember their prey. After a few years you develop your own clues to likely habitat— not sensible food-type indicators like red squirrels but arcane

associations like those used by the hunters of morel mushrooms. For me it is the ground-nesting warbler known as the ovenbird. I have never found a gos nest out of earshot of a singing ovenbird: "teacherteacherTEACHER*TEACHER!*" But let's say you have found a hillside woodlot over running water, with plucking posts and squirrels and ovenbirds and crumbling stick structures, where you are sure that faint "KIKIKI" or "KUKUKU" is not a woodpecker. Don't push too hard—it is easy to frighten a pair of hawks before eggs are laid. Go home and return when, you hope, the young have hatched. Now there is no need for circumspection. Now is the time that the parents attack trail bikes and horses and dogs and elephants. You couldn't dislodge them with dynamite.

Enter the woodlot. Soon, if you have guessed right, you'll see an ominous silhouette stroking along under the canopy, twisting and turning and crying alarm. If you are near the nest she'll turn back toward you again so you can see her fluffy white undertail and know for sure that she is a gos and not some mundane "frog hawk" like the shy broad-wing or whistling red-shoulder. Now the parents will play you an unwilling game of hot and cold as you approach, pass, retreat. Are you getting colder? The voices will fade and the birds will vanish. Hotter? Maybe now you will be able to distinguish two separate voices, the male's high-pitched, and distant, the female's a deeper and more intimidating "KUK." Very hot? Now you will be able to see the red eyes, pearly barred breast, and manic white eyebrow of the bird that courses back and forth, sits screaming, then rushes straight at your face like a hit-and-run driver. Duck!

And she shoots past, a foot overhead. *Where is the damn nest?* As she lands screaming and turns for another run, your eyes catch a black mass in a maple fork twenty-five feet up, a vaguely cone-shaped bulk that looks as big as your body. Oh, *there!* A quick glassing (you duck as she rushes through again) reveals no visible young. Hmm... May 20. Let's try again in a week.

And you do. And maybe you are still too early, and you climb up, under determined attack, to find only eggs. Or you are too late and find the remains of a raccoon's meal, or even a sleeping raccoon.* Or, finally, you might be lucky and find a ten-day-old "downy" ripe for the taking.

A CHILD CAN reach a goshawk's nest—it is the woodland skill needed to find the site that takes time, experience, teaching. Falcons' nests are not hard to see if there are any around at all. Falcons nest on sheer cliffs, on bare rock, on scenic mountains, and over water. Their surroundings are National Geographic-pretty and romantic, but unless you're a rock climber getting to them can be daunting.

I found my first big falcon's nest on the first day I ever looked for one. Nobody, not ever in the world, has done that with an accipiter's nest. We were staying with Harry McElroy, a Texas-born educational psychologist and master falconer, in the northern Nevada mining town of Battle Mountain. Early in our visit Harry suggested that we drive up the "Hilltop" trail out of town to see a little of the local wildlife.

A trail out of town—well, actually more like where the main road petered out against the mountain. Northern Nevada is one of my favorite places in the world, not least because there are no paved roads other than the interstate outside the towns, and the towns are eighty miles apart. The land is enormous, flat broad basins alternating with north-south walls of cold mountain, full of wildlife that comes right up to the edges of the towns. In early spring the sage is dotted with playas—little, shallow, mineral-

---

*Falconers generally fasten a tin collar to any nest tree after they climb it in order that no 'coon will follow their scent to a meal.

rich lakes full of avocets and courting ducks. Despite this water, and the snow on all the ridges, dust devils stride along in the distance like science-fiction monsters.

And hawks are everywhere. As we drove in from California we saw prairies in the medians, Cooper's hawks in the cottonwoods, roughlegs and harriers and eagles in the basins. I mentioned this to Harry. He nodded and advised that if we went up "Hilltop" we might see a hawk or two. What I didn't realize at the time was that Harry is the kind of Texan given to almost British understatement rather than to hyperbole.

Next morning we drove up a rutted dirt track that followed a stream into the Shoshone Range. There was plenty of vegetation in the ravine, but only ankle-high scrub above. The water was swift-flowing and cold—Harry had mentioned trout—and it occasionally swept across the road. We passed the holes of more than one abandoned mine, and once a converted school bus whose owners were picking over a pile of tailings. After fording the stream twice we decided to stop in favor of walking. Apart from the fact that it was easier to see animals while on foot, the trail ahead looked too steep even for four-wheel drive.

Though we weren't five miles out of town there were magpie nests in the alders, toads trilling in the puddles, ravens diving and croaking, deer tracks in the road. A Cooper's hawk, a haggard with a beautiful blue-gray back and a breast barred with robin red, worked a contour just above us, alternately flapping and gliding. Whistles ringing back and forth from the ledges above our heads announced the presence of marmots.

The first indication that there was something more exciting around came from our spaniel, Spud. He had been splashing in and out of the creek and pushing through streamside thickets as if he expected to flush something. I thought I knew what he was smelling. "Watch it," I said to Betsy, "Here comes a deer." And an owl fluttered crazily up out of the tangle like an enormous moth, only to flop down again as soon as it cleared the tops of the bushes. Spud ran in again, but the owl refused to break cover. We could see it staring back in what we imagined was horror, all cartoon-yellow eyes and close-set eyebrows.

Betsy spoke for both of us: "Why won't it fly?" I had no answer. We called off the dog and started down the trail. We hadn't gone fifty feet when Betsy whirled and pointed. "What's that?"

"That" was the reason for the owl's terror, a female prairie falcon landing on a ledge above us. A moment later the tiercel landed on her and they mated. We watched as he balanced, flapping, on her back. Before we could say a thing he finished, rose into the air, and slid smoothly down the wind for fifty yards to fetch up on a sunny ledge where he flopped in apparent contentment. From the next ridge behind him came the steady thump of mining machinery. "Could it be...?" Betsy whispered. I thought it was possible, but didn't dare hope that finding a nest was quite that easy.

"We'll ask Harry."

He seemed pleased but not too surprised. "Might be—we'll go check it out. Got another I want to look at, too, a mile out of town on the other side." We set out in his go-anywhere hawk wagon, a "Baja Bug" that sported a shelf perch where the passenger's grab bar had been and solid paint on the rear side windows to minimize distractions. In true western style and in defiance of gravity and good sense, we drove right up to the site. Harry was actually beginning to look enthusiastic. "When I get on a nest," he assured me in Nevada's slowest drawl, "*you can't stop me!*" As we climbed out he added, "If there's anything here we'd better get out pretty fast. It's too early to hang around much." Within seconds he spotted sign. "Look. Noodles." I hadn't the slightest idea what he was talking about. I peered desperately into the setting sun but before I could see a thing he was backing the bug around, spitting gravel, crunching sage, driving away.

Harry had been oblivious to my ignorance, but when he remembered my eastern background he began to expound. "Noodles," he repeated. "It looks like spaghetti." I had been looking for "whitewash" since we hit the west and had in fact seen some large white splotches. But I had been all wrong. Those splotches had possibly been ravens' or buteos' or even eagles' nests, but not falcons'. Now I was reminded of an elementary fact of raptor physiology. Most birds of prey shoot their liquid droppings a flat six feet on the horizontal. But falcons just dribble straight down. "Noodles," Harry repeated. "Once you see it you won't mistake it for anything else. You'll see."

I TOOK WHAT I had gleaned from Harry back to my new home in southwestern New Mexico. It was a time of shifting perspectives. I could expect to find goshawks within ten miles of anywhere that I had lived in Massachusetts, but in New Mexico I soon found myself checking out "nearby" canyons that were eighty miles away over unspeakable roads. Nests were farther apart than in Nevada, perhaps because water was scarcer, and I had little luck. I found a couple of abandoned but pretty definite nest ledges etched with the distinctive noodles even after a year or more of abandonment. I visited a known site with two falconers from Albuquerque, Jim Skidmore and Mark Slifka, but miles of tramping across rangeland and up the rocky sides of canyons found us a lone female in place—a widow perhaps, but definitely not nesting that year. The whole area within a hundred-mile radius seemed empty of young falcons.

Then, with about five days left in the legal season for taking eyases, I decided to take a last pass by a line of cliffs fifty miles northwest of my home. It was a habitat that only a predator could love: a curl of smoothly sculptured limestone like a breaking wave running for several miles above the desert's harshest landscape, lava "malpais." The lower stratum resembled a titanic bulldozed parking lot, but what looked like tar had the consistency of broken glass. And yet there was life everywhere. Canyon wrens scuttled around the rocks like lizards, bursting into startling loud song, rabbits flushed from underfoot and disappeared under pack-rat nests, fresh deer tracks lingered in the shade of junipers, and colonies of hundreds of white-throated swifts wheeled and screeched overhead in an aerial roller derby. My friends had told me that at least one pair of prairies nested there every year, and they had drawn me a detailed map showing the eyrie. But although I had found nests of raven and redtail I had not seen even a wandering falcon.

Yet something about the area—its innumerable potholes, abandoned nests, and tantalizing possibilities—kept me coming back. That day I spotted, in a deep bay of the cliffs, a stick nest that I hadn't seen before. More out of naturalist's curiosity than from any real expectation I stepped out of the pickup to glass the nest without the vibration of the engine. I could hear a raven's gargle over the truck's noise—and maybe something else. Gesturing "turn it off" to Betsy with one hand, I stepped a little closer to the cliffs, mouth open to catch the faintest sound, hardly daring to believe what I had heard: two unmistakable baby falcon voices screaming alarm, one pitched lower than the other.

For two hours that was all I had. I could see nothing to mark the nest: no movement, no certain noodles, and too many shapeless splashes of whitewash to indicate anything intelligible. The babies sang out more or less continually, but echoes bounding off the walls of the bay made it impossible even to guess where they were. I decided to go up top.

I am no rock climber, and hanging around on top of high walls

is not my favorite part of falconry. You might even consider me a little acrophobic. But I had no choice. I found a place where old rockfalls had opened a possible way to the top and scrabbled up over fifteen-foot pebbles hoping I wouldn't have to turn back. A curve in the rock cut off the sound of the eyases. Somehow I reached the juniper scrub at the top and picked my way cauti-

ously through the last of the level ground—at the last abandoned nest I had explored I had confronted a five-foot diamondback at eye level—to find that the top just curved away exactly like a wave, getting steeper and steeper until it broke. I didn't dare get too far out, and the overhang concealed everything. Impasse.

Finally I forced myself out on one arm of the bay. There

erosion had produced an arch and some fissures where I could theoretically get down a little and look back into the curve. I could see some observation ledges just below me, whitened with what looked like falcon droppings. Now I could see Betsy below, looking sickeningly tiny and foreshortened, and once again hear the nervous chant of at least two little falcons. There was nothing to do but edge out even farther. I flattened out on my belly and crawled.

It was horrible. I was angled head down, and I could feel the cliff tilting to spill me off. The only biting gnats I have yet encountered in New Mexico swarmed around my sweating face. And white-throated swifts, doubtless drawn by the gnats, zoomed by a foot from my face at about sixty miles an hour, so fast that their wings hummed. I forced myself forward until I could see bare ledge spattered with whitewash and hear the babies as clearly as if they were amplified. I *still* couldn't see the eyrie. In the circumstances all I could do was retreat. I crawled back, stood and just breathed for about ten minutes before my legs would support me well enough for the climb back.

When I reached the foot of the talus slope Betsy ran up to inform me that the birds must be able to see her. Every time she moved, they screeched. Before I could give her any all-knowing falconer's remarks I looked up toward the noise once more. And there, in a pothole that was invisible from more than ten feet away in either direction, stood two nearly fledged prairie falcons like little mannequins. Screaming.

WE RETURNED the next day with Jim and Mark. They arrived equipped with ropes and climbing equipment, assuring me that rock climbing was easy. They had already decided that Jim would go down the rope and Mark would man the cliff top and handle the belaying. Not only did I not have to dangle over the edge of the precipice, but I could watch the whole thing. And if the eyases flew, as was more than likely considering their age, I would be the one to run them down.

"If we're lucky they'll fly first, before we even have to rope down." Jim, now in charge, gave Betsy and me our last briefing before he went up. "I'll throw the rope over first. Give me a tug when it touches the ground. Betsy can man the bottom end. You get out there at the bottom of the talus slope where you can see their flight if they go." His brisk commands were punctuated by the rhythmic "kikikiks" of the eyases.

It took them three quarters of an hour to reach the top, using the same route I had taken. Meanwhile Betsy scrambled up the talus slope to a ledge where it met the cliff face and I watched the sights. The old female glided in, calling, and landed on one of the lookout posts where she sat fat and placid, with one foot tucked up. A raven drifted by, croaking. A flock of swifts screeched around the corner of the bluff. The brilliant high-country sun made everything shiny and almost too bright to watch until, despite the anticipation, I almost dozed off. Then a whisper of sound reached my ears. Two insects on the cliff top were waving and shouting.

Something about the acoustics of the cliff made it impossible for Betsy to hear them, so I had to relay their shouted instructions, the first of which was for her to take cover.

"Take cover!"

"What?"

"Get in the cave!" (me)

Betsy: "I can't hear them!"

Everybody: "GET IN THE CAVE!"

Seconds later, a whole dead pinyon slid over the edge and crashed down. When the echoes died I nervously called, "Are you all right?"

"I can't hear you."

"ARE YOU ALL RIGHT?"

Jim and Mark abandoned the idiot attempts at communication for their next act, which was to toss a banner of beer cans and orange flagging over the edge on a rope and jingle it in the eyrie's mouth in hopes of spooking the children into their first flight. Instead of flying they shrieked and ran to the back of the cave. It was time to go over. But there was one problem not easily visible from below. The reason I had been unable to see the nest was that there was an overhang. We decided I would go up to Betsy's station at the top of the talus slope, where I'd swing Jim on the rope like the clapper on a bell until he could get purchase on the ledge.

Betsy started down over the boulders. Calm Jim, impatient as anyone now that the moment was at hand ("You *can't stop me!*") dropped over the edge and started to swing himself in ten foot arcs before I could even reach the rope. The shrieking reached a new crescendo, the old female stroked across the cliff face, adding to the din, and as Jim attempted to hook his boot heel on the ledge, first one, then the other little tiercel flew. The first went right, the second (as I raced down the slope chasing the first) left. Things became frantic. I have a confused mental image of madly flapping young birds erupting like flushing quail, of Jim spinning as he kicks ineffectually at the wall, and of Betsy, halfway down the talus slope, shouting, "THERE IT GOES OVER THERE, IT'S STILL FLYING!" while all the time the alarm shrieks continue to come from the next ledge. Then Jim somehow managed to get his foothold.

"You're not going to believe this. There are still two in here!"

"Falcons?" (Me, hoping for a hawk large enough to take grouse.)

"No, tiercels. A nest full of tiercels. And these two are still downy."

We decided to leave the little ones alone. Jim came down the rope to aid in the search. We found the "number two" tiercel in five minutes, panting like a dog from his first flight. He sat owlishly upright in the grass until Jim picked him up and put him into the air-conditioned car. We still hoped the first flyer might be a falcon rather than a tiercel. Besides, even if he were the tiercel he appeared to be we had to get him off the ground and back to his parents before night brought its coyotes and owls.

I spotted him watching us from a fallen boulder, but he flew again and vanished into a slope of shrubbery and tumbled rocks. We made a line up the slope, which was covered by a miserable tangle of cholla and juniper and yucca, and began a detailed examination of the terrain. Since Jim insisted that the bird could hide under a rock we had to look into every likely rattlesnake den that we passed.

We searched for hours. And hours. I had convinced myself that this bird was a female, decided in a sudden reversal that I wanted a male, and therefore only half wanted to find it. This of course spurred my conscience and made me search even harder. A raven, apparently about the same age as the hawks, flapped clumsily to a boulder top muttering adolescent defiance. Its mother circled anxiously overhead, croaking and gargling her distress until she attracted the attention of two kestrels who came out to harass her, taking turns stooping and screeching as she protested: "Kleekleekleekleeklee! . . . Rhaagh . . . rlaagh!"

We quit the slopes as the shadows grew long and walked the grassy bottom. Suddenly the fourth indisputable tiercel materialized, sitting on a boulder again, watching our approach. I circled behind him while Jim stalked in with weary care, making magician's passes in the air to mesmerize him. When we were three feet away we both made dives at his feet. Jim connected, and in a second I held my very first big native longwing, furious and shining and still bearing wisps of natal down.

We decided to keep him instead of his brother; he had flown farther. We got the other bird out of the car and climbed the talus to the foot of the sheer cliff. Jim propped the remaining hunk of pinyon below a pothole eight feet up the face, swarmed up it and slam-dunked the bird into the hole. He dropped and we ducked, hoping the bird would remain in that relatively safe spot at least until morning. Just as we were beginning to relax, he bolted out over our heads. This time he caught the evening updraft and soared to a pinnacle three quarters of the way up the face, safer than we could have made him. As he flew we could see the old tiercel had joined the screaming falcon crossing and recrossing above.

"What happened? What's all the commotion?"

"You wouldn't believe it if I told you."

4

"There be some sports are painful, and their labor
Delight in them sets off."
—Ferdinand, in *The Tempest*

H E WAS a ten-day-old male lanner, and I thought he was just
perfect. He wasn't pretty—just a scrawny, pot-bellied,
barely birdlike creature covered with thin white down. I picked
him up and he rocked back on his hindquarters like a clumsy toy,
oversize feet projecting out in front on legs as yet too weak to
support his weight. His head wobbled around in a half circle as
though it were on a spring, searching my thumbs for a meal. His
weight and deep heat were startling, out of proportion with his
starling-size body. I was in love.

During the two-hour drive from breeder Tom Ricardi's to my
apartment I had time to think about all the alternative methods
and theories of bird training, time for the first high euphoria to
wear off and be replaced by worry. The bright-eyed, frog-faced
thing that sat beside me in the box was not just a baby hawk but a
tabula rasa for me to make or mar. He was only the third eyas I
had ever trained, though about the tenth bird—and neither of
the other young birds had been outstanding successes. And
finally, he was my first big longwing.

Orthodox opinion has always recommended as little contact
with eyases as possible. The theory was the contact bred famil-

iarity, contempt, and screaming. The falconer would turn his bird loose in a shed, only coming in to feed her once a day. He would tie her food to a "hack board" and leave. When she was "hard penned"—that is, when her feathers were all full-grown —he would withhold food for a day and then turn her loose. He would then place food on the hack board and put the board somewhere in plain sight. Theoretically such a program would lead the bird to develop strong flight muscles and good hunting habits. The first time she missed a meal the falconer would set a bow net at the hack board and take her up for training.

Although "hacking" did produce strong birds its other results were usually less than spectacular. A bird handled this way was fearful enough to demand a lot of training and handling, yet bold enough to retain aggression. While she might not scream immediately she usually started as soon as you cut down her meat

intake to overcome her stubborn refusal to fly to your lure or your glove. A few heretics, notably Ronald Stevens in Ireland and Harry McElroy in the United States, decided that if a school of thought still produced lousy results after a thousand years, perhaps a new way doing things should be considered. Both ultimately wrote entire books concerned largely with the handling of infant birds: Steven's *Observations on Modern Falconry* and McElroy's *Desert Hawking*. At the risk of oversimplifying, I can boil down their detailed instructions on rearing to two principles: no hunger and lots of pleasant contact.

"Gremlin's" progress was gratifying and very much according to the book. At the time I was working as a rodman on a state survey crew. Every morning I would load Gremlin, his shallow box full of newspaper, and a cooler full of food and drive to my job. He would ramble cheerfully around inside my '72 Hornet all day, streaking the upholstery with hawk chalk, filling the air with starling feathers and wisps of molting down. My fellow workers spent half their time around the car, talking to him in tones usually reserved for puppies and very small children. I had to watch them to make sure they didn't feed him any hot dogs. Every hour or so I'd pop an oversized hood over his head and leave it in place for about thirty seconds. He rarely so much as flinched.

I was determined that he would never see any food in my hand—the biggest cause of screaming is this early association— so I would dismember his day-old cockerels and lab mice or dust his beef with bonemeal and place them in a dish. Then I would bring him to the dish. After a moment he would discover the food, stump over to it like a man with two wooden legs, and fall on it. Pretty soon he would be sitting back up on his tail again, a chick's foot projecting out of his mouth like a cigar, his crop as round as a golf ball.

I let him stay on the job until he began to rise from the seat when he flapped. Since I did not want to shut the windows and cook him, I began to leave him home. When I returned in the evening he would run up to me on the floor like a dog, or sit in the dingy apartment window turning his head entirely upside down in a hawk's alarming gesture of greeting. If I stood still he would fly to my hand, then hop to my shoulder to end up on my head.

Rather than feed him right away, I would often drive to my father's house in the country, where he could roam a large fenced yard at liberty. Now that he was starting to fly I began to feed him on the lure, that bird-shaped device of cloth or leather that you use as a silent dinner bell to call your hawk. I still did not let him see me tie the food to the lure, but made it up in the house while he chased butterflies out back. When I tossed the lure onto the lawn he would come running. And I mean *running*, not flying, although he sometimes spread his wings as he came in, gliding in short bounces.

But this kind of "tame hack" is best carried on in less enclosed areas. One windy day he became airborne about twenty feet away and with no warning shied around me at the last moment. As I turned he climbed the wind in a long arc and disappeared around the corner of the house. It took me ten of the longest minutes of my life before I found him sitting on a neighbor's roof. I ran to the open lawn and threw the lure down, whistling for his attention. He ignored me and scanned the horizon, panting from exertion. I yelled "HO!" and threw it down again, praying that habit would bring him in despite the fact that he was as fat as a butterball turkey. This time he looked at me. On my third throw he bobbed his head, took off, and glided down. He landed three feet from the lure, ran over, and hit it as if it were a tackling dummy. As he folded his wings I started to breathe again. It was time to start training in earnest.

THE TRAINING of any hawk is the most important and the most frustrating part of falconry. Training can be defined as what goes on between the time you first get a hawk in your hands and the time that you take your first head of game together, or, more poetically, as the forging of that bond that allows you to aid each other in the hunt. You must always remember that you do not teach her to kill; you teach her to return, and to accept you as her servant.

Because the bond is central to the training process the education of an imprint eyas is relatively painless—she already loves you. Of course, you'll have to help her learn to fly. She may prefer as Gremlin did to run to you rather than to risk her untried wings. If you toss her into the air she may flutter down and sit owlishly staring at you. And although she will have the basic instinct to chase and kill other creatures, she will entirely lack the skills. Such naïveté can be gruesome—after watching a few nestlings bungle "bagged" kills early in my falconry career, I decided that though it might help them, it bothered me. Very young hawks tend to start eating before the prey is dead. Baby falcons will properly bite at their quarry's head, but once they have made the effort, they seem to feel that the job is done, and will commence feeding even if the prey is still squawking. I now postpone their introduction to live food until they are strong and good at "footing."

But despite her innocent cruelty, an imprint is easy to get along with. For real difficulty try a traditional eyas or, better still, a passage bird. Go into the hawk house where your new captive sits leashed to her perch in the dark. As you approach she will tighten down every feather except for those that frame her head and flare in a sunburst around her staring eyes and half-open beak to make her look savage rather than terrified. Then she is off the perch in an arrested leap faster than a rattlesnake's strike, wings beating so fast you blink and wince despite yourself. Then up again, hissing defiance, wings half spread. You bring your fist up with unbearable deliberation behind her ankles, where your touch makes her step back to your glove involuntarily. She realizes you are touching her and she "bates"—leaps—again. You unfasten her leash with your ungloved hand as you swing her clear of the perch, wind the leash behind her back as she dangles upside down, full of horror and hatred. You push her gently up until she lies across your glove as if paralyzed, feet hanging, and rock your fist until she scrambles to her feet. For a moment she stands erect on your glove with a look that resembles disbelief on her face. Then she hurls herself off again, to hang, to be helped up, to bate again. And bate, and bate, and bate.

It can take anything from a few hours to a few weeks to get through this harrowing stage. Some hawks, like merlins, are naturally easy, some—passage prairies and goshawks come to mind—are almost impossibly hardheaded. Of course, the more different hawks you handle the better an intuitive handler you will be. If you can anticipate a bate and forestall it by a movement, an offered tidbit, or even by stopping the session, both you and the hawk will be better off—the hawk because action causes and reinforces fright and flight as well as the other way around, and you because you will not be driven to drink, drugs, or raptoricide. Bating is maddening for the falconer because it is both mindless and startling. If it goes on for weeks, it is probable that you are doing something wrong or you have hold of a very dubious bird. In either case, you both might be better off if you, as the old falconers said, "whistle her down the wind."

The best course is not to constantly keep the bird on your fist, although the Arabs do and the medieval falconers did. They have an endless supply of hawks and an endless supply of servants, and even so such a regimen is brutally hard on man and bird. Far better to spend a few minutes every morning and every evening doing pleasant things like feeding your charge a hunk of bloody, feathery meat. For the first day or so she may not eat, though she'll want to. She will shift her feet uneasily, cock an eye downward, perhaps even open and shut her beak several times in a way that suggests that her mouth is watering. At such a moment the temptation to sort of point to the meat, to indicate that it's there, may be overwhelming. But if you do she will probably bate again. Even worse than waving your hands around at foot level is to bring your hand up garnished with a tidbit. A gos will grab you, which is likely to unveil new vistas in pain. Any other hawk, unaccustomed to seeing meat glide in at beak height, will rear and hiss and, at last, bate. And bate. And ignore the meat for many more minutes.

At the end of the second day you will be convinced that she's starving. (She won't be.) Knowing that hawks are supposed to be shy of the human face, you hold her at chest level and fix your eyes at the opposite wall. You wiggle your fingers inside the glove that she stands on. She dips her head slightly; perhaps the stirring beneath her feet reminds her of a not-quite-dead prey animal. She dips it again. Is she feeding? You *can't see.* You lift your hand—just an inch—and lower your gaze.

She bates.

You go through the whole process again. This time you hear the sticky meat tearing. She shakes her head irritably to rid it of a clinging feather. You raise her up so slowly that you can barely control the movement. Her head comes up. You hold this tableau for a very long thirty seconds. She takes another bite, then stops again.

Infinitely slowly you reach out your bare hand and tweak one of her toes. She bites at it viciously, bites again at the meat, and begins to feed. Avidly, voraciously, as though she hadn't eaten in weeks. You return her to the perch just as she finishes, moving at the rate of 16 RPM, smoothing every muscular twitch and fighting an irrational urge to jump and yell. She steps easily to the perch in an absentminded way, as though she had done it a hundred times before. She strops her bill on the perch— "feaks"—and rouses until she looks like a ball of feathers, shaking them down with a clatter like a wet dog. You slip out, full of victory, grinning.

And the next day you go through the whole battle again.

Then, almost overnight, she will begin to look forward to your visits. In her simple world, you mean food and perhaps also a release from boredom. Now you begin to jump her to the fist, or perhaps, if she is a longwing, to the lure. This part of training can edge toward comedy. She wants the food, but for some reason she does not want to fly. She sidles back and forth on her perch, stamping her feet, craning her neck forward, again and again. She half-spreads her wings; yes! this time she'll surely go! But she furls them and begins her idiot dance again.

Then, so suddenly she takes you both by surprise, she's off the perch. If it is your hand she lands on, she may bate off in horror at her own audacity. If it is the lure, she will most likely just stand there for long moments, even minutes. If she is an older eyas she may well mantle over the lure or your hand like an umbrella. But sooner or later she will begin to feed. *She has come back to you.*

I T IS EASY to get used to a miracle. In two days you both treat the whole process as a routine exercise. You whistle, she flies to the lure, she feeds, you pick her up. Perhaps you reward her with a tidbit. You practice your routine, doing it two or three times in a row, but you don't repeat it so many times that she gets bored.

Now you must go outside, to the hawk's familiar surroundings, a world of color and space and, above all, distractions. You tie her leash to her perch and retreat inside, where you watch her through the nearest window. At first she shows an amazing

stupidity about her perch. Although it is the only thing within reach she can comfortably stand on she bates away from it, hopping up and down at the end of her leash like a tormented junkyard dog. Then, suddenly—hawks' changes of mood, of idea, of whatever mind they have, are always startling—she will turn around, hop to the perch, fluff her feathers, and stand on one foot. Instant contentment.

It is feeding time, or maybe, for safety's sake, a little later. You go out and produce the lure (garnished with some really tempting tidbit like half a pigeon or a whole feathered quail) from behind your back like a magician at a kid's party. Ta-da! You throw it at her feet, an easy two feet from her perch.

She looks at the horizon.

You tug on the string and whistle.

She turns her head, looks through you, and stares at another compass point.

You repeat your action. She comes back from whatever planet she has been on, sees the lure, and acknowledges it by bobbing her head. By now you're talking, coaxing: "C'mon girl, *food*, c'mon, here it is, pretty baby..."

She turns her back to you and bates. You turn your back and swear, or cry, or threaten suicide, or vow to go and get your ten-gauge magnum shotgun and blow the feathered demon to hell. You do it very quietly. Then you turn back and whistle. "C'mon, girl."

She bounces up and down two more times at her tether's end, then turns and hops to the perch. She lowers her head and stares at the lure. "Oh, food!" She leaps onto it with every appearance of pleasure and begins to eat.

In three days she dispenses with the preliminary bating and leaps to the lure at your whistle. You are ready for the creance. The creance is nothing more than a long leash. Some brave or fatalistic falconers dispense with it entirely—and some, like me, feel that the natural tendency of the line to hang up on any surface rougher than a golf course makes it at best a necessary evil, to be used no more than once or twice.

If you use your creance skillfully, the hawk will never know she is doing anything but flying freely to you. As the years go by you will become more and more careful about details. You won't avoid just obvious hazards like trees and overhead wires; you will get picky about even grass tussocks. Rather than tying the end of the cord to a stationary object that will bring up an errant bird with a jerk, you will devise ingenious rolling drags and play her down like a fish or a delicate kite. And after once enduring the laborious retraining steps you must use after frightening a bird on the creance—you might consider this event ten steps backward if you just have to pick her out of the grass, or about thirty if she hangs up—you will do it right.

Now comes the single scariest moment in falconry. When your hawk comes one hundred yards on the creance, you've got to TURN HER LOOSE! The earlier steps can be frustrating, or even maddening, but having survived them it goes against your nature to take this being that you've spent so much time on and simply throw her away. If the bird is an eyas, you have a responsibility as well; you know she cannot survive on her own. You wait for the perfect psychological and even physiological moment, when you *know* rather than think that nothing can go wrong, then go out with lead feet, short breath, and a heavy heart, feeling as if you are walking to your execution.

And the bird flies promptly to your fist and begins to eat. The bond is made.

I would like to tell you that this moment is one of the most memorable events in a falconer's life, but in fact your bird's first free flight is usually a single step in the middle of a long journey. You remember the apprehension rather than the relief. It is just like stepping backward over a cliff face on your first rappelling lesson, or maybe like taking your first parachute jump—impossible, then suddenly so easy that you wonder why you didn't do it a week or a season before.

In fact, it is a little too easy to become overconfident at this stage. If your bird is a falcon, especially a merlin or a prairie or a gyr, you may go out the next day and toss her into the air, hoping reasonably enough that she will circle back expecting a meal on her lure. What will most likely happen is that she will fly straight away and disappear over the horizon. Unless you have a good transmitter you will never see her again. Peregrines and buteos may kill from a circling soar, but these falcons fly low over open country, hoping to flush their quarry at short range. She wasn't running away, just hunting; small consolation as she turns into a vibrating dot in the distance. What you should do for a long time with such a bird is call her toward you, or from a friend's fist, until you are sure that she understands the drill.

N OW COMES a period of consolidation. If your bird is a redtail or goshawk you may just do a series of exercises, tossing her up, calling her down, letting her chase the lure, encouraging her to descend from taller and taller trees. But if you have a falcon, taking a little time out for pure play, for an advanced "tame hack," will do you both more good than any rigorous program of work. You just let her fly around at will. Ethologists do not consider falcons especially intelligent, but I wonder. Their capacity for aerial acrobatics and foolery is matched only by the clowning of ravens, and they seem to fly for the pure hell of it, unlike, for instance, the dour goshawk.

Gremlin's first exercise yard was an athletic field in the suburbs, big enough to contain three baseball diamonds and a running track, but a little cramped for a sixteen-ounce adolescent falcon. At first I would nervously call him in to the lure if he showed any sign of straying beyond the trees at the field's edge. However, after one harrowing incident during which he flew to the downtown area five miles away, he learned to stay inside the park. (He homed in on me as I stood in a sidewalk phone booth frantically summoning falconers to the search; I think he was at least as glad to see me as I was to see him, and the look on the faces of the sidewalk strollers when I emerged from the phone booth with Gremlin on my fist tearing at a chicken leg almost made the terror worthwhile.)

His first act on leaving my fist was always to patrol the field's perimeter looking for dogs. It wasn't exactly that he didn't like dogs—he had been raised with them—but more as though he got some kind of unholy joy out of harassing them. He would dive down and swat a dog on the rump, then pass it and fly away three feet above the ground. When the dog—inevitably—gave chase, he would toss up, turn over, and hit it again. After a few passes the dog would usually retreat and he would come back up the wind to me.

People also drew his attention, though, unless they were walking dogs, not his aggression. A lot of them never seemed to so much as see him, although a few ran headlong out of the field. Pretty soon I would glass the entire field for tempting targets and curious onlookers before I let him go. Even if he didn't buzz them I got tired of the questions, one of the most common being, "Is that thing *real?*" Wild birds were another, more serious diversion. He caught his first one when he spiraled down around a light standard as though it were a maypole and nailed a sparrow at its base in a cloud of dust. After that, he would take an aerial stand over any small bird that he saw, pinning it down in the bleachers or the trash barrels like a pointer until I could run in and flush it. Starlings and pigeons were another story. Following a few fruitless tail chases he realized that they could attain the trees and houses at the field's edge before he could. After that he mostly ignored them, though sometimes he would fly wing to wing, almost companionably, with a passing pigeon. Crows, the only other common bird in the park, terrified the little hawk. He would fly away from them as they dived and cawed, dodging and flaring until his nervous pursuers decided that they had pressed their luck long enough.

When he was strong and confident on the wing I began to teach him in earnest. Until this time I had let him wander where he pleased, only calling him to the lure if he looked as if he were about to leave the field. Now we began a new game. I would show him the lure when he began to circle, but as soon as he came in I'd hide it behind my back. He would sky up in surprise, looking back over his shoulder. At which point I'd hang the lure out in the air again. He'd fold up and stoop at it. If he tagged it I would let go; if not, I'd pull it back and he would climb again. We had begun field training.

F IELD TRAINING is like "yard training" in a larger arena, with more skills laid on. Some of the objectives, such as return and control, are exactly the same; some, like hunting and flying skills, are new. Shortwingers do not do much field training. Their birds' talents are best honed in direct pursuit. And fliers of passage falcons, knowing that their birds can already hunt and kill, probably do too little, passing right by control on the way to the excitements of the hunt. Though their haste is understandable, a little patience at this point can bring the falconer great rewards in pleasure and confidence. A hawk that waits on overhead is more visible and less nerve-racking than one that soars in circles a mile downwind or that checks away at game that she has spotted beyond the horizon. And one that stoops a thousand feet is more spectacular than one that stoops a hundred, as well as more deadly.

I was teaching Gremlin two sets of skills useful for a quail and small bird hawk. First, I wanted him to stay right over my head even if I moved, and to make tight circles over the place where the game put in, even if it took a while to dislodge it. Second, I wanted him to have good wind in case he had to make a series of attacks. Once he caught on to the game I would encourage him to chase the lure through fifty or more pendulum-swing short stoops, until he began to open his mouth and pant. Then I would let go and let him catch it. Sometimes he would strike up at the lure like a goshawk; other times he would bind to it and fly it to the ground, or cut at it repeatedly, strafing it until it was "dead." Finally he would stand astride his toy, proud and winded, guarding it until he got his breath back and began to eat the meat that I had tied on for his reward.

Such exercise is necessary and sufficient for a lanneret. Too much height is a disadvantage when you are hunting small birds that fly for short distances near the ground. But such a regimen would ruin a true game hawk or one that was to be flown at ducks. A hawk that is destined for large strong-flying open-country game must wait on not only precisely but also, above all, *high* above the falconer.

I KNOW of no one more expert in teaching hawks to wait on than Jim Skidmore, a forty-year-old Albuquerque resident with a neat mustache and precise habits. Jim owns a fourteen-year-old pre-act passage peregrine, three Elhew pointers, and the complete works of Elbert Hubbard, author of "A Message to Garcia." His elaborate training waltzes, conducted on eleven unfenced sections of grassland west of the city, are more elegant and demanding than most people's hunts. And yet he correctly regards them as mere maneuvers, rigorous drills calculated to produce hawks capable of taking prairie grouse with style and consistency.

Jim's theories are eccentric. He thinks that most hawks get too much of the wrong kind of exercise, and except when he's actually hunting he prefers to fly his birds only once or twice a week so they won't get bored. Many falconers, including myself, dread the moment when a bird gets into a thermal, stretching her wings and fanning her tail. We know that we may never see her again if she succumbs to the temptation to drift with the wind. But Jim believes that thermals and soaring are mere aids to correct waiting on. And his practice drills confirm his theories.

Although those drills can be surreal pageants. On a single Saturday last October we took out three birds in different stages of training. One was a young hybrid undergoing his first season in the "Skidmore Method." The second, Mark Slifka's second-year female prairie falcon, was a sort of graduate student, taking a refresher course after the summer inactivity of the molt. And the third was Jim's wise and ancient peregrine, "Bougain," who had finished her molt just three weeks before and had not even flown since March.

We came through the gates into the open grassland at eight in the morning, an odd western safari composed of three pickup trucks full of dogs, birds, and radio equipment. The first step involved following Jim in a seemingly aimless cross-prairie ramble while he computed endless variables of wind, slope, and I suppose just plain intuition. He would drive for five minutes, stop, glass the empty plain, and go on. Eventually he turned at right angles. We followed, our trucks wallowing on the tussocky ground like small boats in a choppy sea, until we reached the day's "Place." We knew it was "The Place" because Jim, as always, turned in a half circle before he stopped for good. We turned, parked parallel to his truck, and cut our engines. In the gray fall morning the immense brown grassland looked like the sea, rolling and free of landmarks. Only the distant mountains gave us any scale—Sandia Crest running like a blade twenty-odd miles east, beyond Albuquerque,; the Fuji-like cone of Ladron sixty miles south, with the Magdalenas beyond; the Jemez range and Taylor to the north and northwest, already tipped with snow. Longwing country. The only signs of life were a raven on passage half a mile up, and a scatter of fleeing "road larks."

We weren't left much time to contemplate the scene. Jim was already unloading his unique implements from the recesses of his camper. The interior of Jim's truck is a stern admonition to those of us who lead incurably sloppy lives. A lot of people make their own hawk "furniture"—perches, leashes, hoods, blocks.

But very few also make perfectly engineered fittings and boxes to hold them. As you look into Jim's hawk wagon you see a sturdy traveling perch on the left; stacked dog boxes up at the head, each containing an eager but quiet pointer; live-bird boxes; brackets for receiver antennas; a folded mahogany game table in its own holder; a rack for dog chains; and, finally, a drilled two-by-four into which the hawks' block perches fit as though into sockets. The whole outfit is so free of dust, hair, droppings, dead pigeons and other falconry detritus that you feel you could eat off its surfaces.

Jim staked out his dog chain—a heavy central chain with spikes at each end and four short chains spaced along its length that snapped to the dogs' collars. He dealt out four bowls of water, then attached the dogs: pointers Jake and Dot, Mark's Brittany, Harvey, and our young springer spaniel, Maggie. He

set up the felt-topped game table and erected a ring of folding chairs around it, then loaded it with thermoses of coffee, doughnuts, and a single rose in a vase. He took three block perches into the lee of the pickup truck's shelter, rammed their spikes into the soft earth, set a hooded hawk on each, and returned to the coffee table. It was Strategy Time.

Of course, each bird had to be handled differently. By now we had been flying the hybrid "Cedric" and the prairie for several weeks and knew their foibles. Cedric was a combination of prairie and gyr who liked to race around at low altitudes. You had to curb your impulse to serve him until he made an effort to go up. He was a quick study, and had learned the elementary lesson that pointing dog means birds. He had deduced from our refusal to flush his quarry when he flew around at lawnmower level, plus his greater success in killing when he stooped from a good pitch, that it was politic to mount up a little higher every time we went out. I thought of him as "promising."

Mark's prairie needed no help with the mechanical part of flight training. She had taken many head of game in her first year. She would climb, with or without thermals, until she was a speck in the sky, and keep an eye on the dog. Her problem was that she had developed a lazy habit of drifting downwind from the point in search of updrafts. Therefore she often waited on in a position where she was too far away to take advantage of the flush.

Bougain was perfect and wise, but she was still a little fat and very soft.

"Whatever you do, don't release that bird for Ceddy until he goes up." (Jim.)

"Right."

"What about the prairie?" (Me.)

"No problem."

Mark agreed: "She'll remember her business and come back over. We just have to give her a little *time*."

"And the peregrine...?" I was sure that we couldn't do much with her other than call her to the lure. Last week she had refused to jump six feet for it. According to the conventional wisdom, even if she wanted to fly she couldn't carry all her weight very far on slack summer muscles without either giving up or dying of apoplexy.

"She should fly just fine today. She's just about ready." He must have noticed my look of skepticism—I had never seen the bird work. "I know she's a little out of condition but she's smart enough to get up there without working very hard."

Right, I thought. The others should fly well anyway.

As the hybrid was still being a little early-morning-uppity, we decided to fly the prairie first. We took a strong game-farm chukar partridge and what I can only describe as an artful artificial tussock with a thirty-foot string attached and hiked out from the trucks for about half a mile. Jim directed the placement of the "gamebird set" on the crest of a two-foot ridge, placed the chukar under it, then stretched the cord out on its upwind side so that the bird would be naturally placed between the pointer and the flusher. I attempted to memorize every twig, every blade of grass, and every cowflop within twenty feet, trying to avoid the embarrassment of last week when I had delayed the flush with my inability to distinguish the fake tussock from the real ones.

We returned to the truck and released Jake. Jake is what is known as a "big-going" pointer. He bounded upwind with unnerving enthusiasm, covering hundreds of yards with each cast, nose low, tail high and quivering, nose drinking scent. In a moment his casts shortened like a compass needle wobbling to magnetic north. He ran a few steps closer, dropped his head, vibrated, and stopped. Only an almost invisible tremor in his tail betrayed the fact that he was alive.

Mark faced his prairie into the wind. She looked around as though she was bored, then suddenly leaped into the air. Just as we had feared, she curved downwind until she was almost out of sight before she began to climb. We watched her circles through the binoculars. "See that?" said Jim, always the theorist. "She was feeling too lazy to climb, so she's found herself a thermal. That's okay, as long as she comes back over." But she showed no desire to return. We could see her shuttling back and forth in the distance like a bead on a string. She had no desire to go astray; in her eye and her mind she commanded the air around the dog's point. Unfortunately she didn't. Although she could see the flush perfectly well, and probably even manage to kill a game-farm chukar from her pitch, a wild grouse could beat her from that flush without even getting winded. Mark walked in close behind Jake and twirled his glove, the signal to "come in over." She continued her short circles.

So we waited. And waited. Jake's tail vibrated. Harvey, the Brit, whined in his impatience to close with the chukar. The chukar thought whatever thoughts a pen-raised bird under a basket thinks. Finally, after a very long five minutes, the falcon moved in over about half the distance and began to make circles again.

"Close enough," said Mark. He clipped a lead onto the straining Harvey and began to edge around Jake. By the time he got the cord in his hands Harvey was whining and scrabbling, no longer interested in pointing. He wanted to FLUSH NOW! Mark twirled the glove one last time; jerked the string, released Harvey, and hollered, "HAAAAH!"

The bird flushed with a cackle of fright and buzzed off downwind about ten feet above the ground. The prairie slanted down in a long flying stoop, crossed the bird head-on, tagged it hard enough to jerk loose a clot of feathers, and continued flying upward. As the bird hit the grass, the prairie turned, dropped, and rolled it again. She tossed up, hovered, and fell to the ground, where the grass hid the end. When we found her she was already plucking her quarry. Harvey lay at her side, guarding the kill, panting and grinning.

Next came Cedric. When we released him he buzzed around like a big black bat or the damn-fool adolescent he was, "cutting daisies" with his wings, skimming the ground, nearly giving the dog a haircut in a run that would have flushed any wild bird holding in front of the point. When none of his antics produced a reaction he swung out a few hundred yards and began to climb like the gyrfalcon he resembled, clawing his way up at a sharp angle. When Jim twirled his glove he came in at about four hundred feet, soaring on the wind like a kite. His first stoop was a textbook marvel, vertical and close-winged, but he missed his shot. He overhauled the bird in a tail chase, again making use of his gyrfalcon speed, and rode it to the ground. We gave him a B+.

We put out a third set and turned loose Jake, who soon made another classic point. Jim brought out the old peregrine and deftly popped off her hood. She was a big bird, much wider across the shoulders than either of her fellow hunters, with an almost metallic sheen to her feathers that contrasted with their dull fluffiness. She looked placid and domestic. Jim faced her into the wind. She tightened her feathers, gripped down on his glove, and rowed a few practice strokes. Then she stopped, relaxed, and puffed herself up very slowly. But instead of the expected "rouse" she gave an irritable "kack" and closed them up again. Jim stood there, silent, head bowed. She jumped from his fist and lumbered through the air to a point about a hundred feet away, where she lit on the ground.

It was about what I expected. I figured that any hawk needed exercise after the molt before she could fly with any ability at all and I was puzzled by Jim's insistence to the contrary. He was walking away now. Was he angry, or embarrassed? He passed the hawk without giving her so much as a look. After a moment she roused where she stood, bobbed her head in Jim's direction, and took off again. She flew past him and lit on the ground. He kept walking. The third time she took off she passed him, still flying slowly, and continued on. When she got about a quarter mile out she began to climb in big circles, pumping hard. Jim came back grinning. "Let's give Maggie a little flushing practice."

Betsy led Maggie to a position opposite the set from Jake, and after a minute's panic I found the string and handed it to her.

It took me a moment to locate Bougain. She was soaring, no longer climbing, seven or eight hundred feet above but still a quarter mile downwind of us. Jim stood watching, holding his glove down by his side. "That's amazing," I called, acknowledging her ability. "Aren't you ready yet?"

He shook his head. "She's just resting. She'll go up a *lot* higher than that. And come in a lot closer. Whatever you do, *don't flush yet.*"

Sure enough, in a moment she commenced to climb again. At a distance hard to estimate but well over a thousand feet she stopped circling and soared forward for the second time. Now she was closer. Before I could ask Jim anything I saw a raven edge in from the side at about the same altitude. For two minutes the two birds circled for advantage like enemy fighter planes. Then the raven slid away on a descending arc to the east and the peregrine resumed her circling.

She climbed two more aerial steps while I watched, open-mouthed. By the time she reached the second bench she was no longer in clear sight from the ground. She was just a dot going in and out of thin clouds; the spots in my eyes were clearer. Keeping my eyes on the speck I raised my binoculars. Through them she was just perceptibly bird-shaped. Without dropping my gaze I hollered to Jim: "Now?"

He was swinging his tracking antenna, having lost sight of her when he checked the point, and twirling his glove. I could see the motion in my peripheral vision.

"How about when she gets just exactly above you?"

Betsy muttered, "I haven't been able to see her for five minutes."

"Just pull the string when my binoculars go past vertical." The hawk was coming forward even as I made the suggestion. "Now!" Betsy tugged the string. I looked down in spite of myself even though I knew I'd lose sight of the bird. The spaniel ran in attempting to catch the chukar that crouched, stupidly, almost too long, then clattered into the air. "HAAAH! HAAAH!"

And I looked up to see a dot dropping, becoming an inverted heart, a diving bird. The wind screamed through her bells, making a sound like nothing else on earth as she fell a half-mile through the clear autumn air. At the last moment she turned parallel to the chukar's line of flight and hit it from behind with the solid "thwack" of a large-caliber bullet striking flesh. The air filled with a blizzard of feathers as the chukar fell boneless from the sky. The falcon made a delicate curve in the air, turned, and landed on the fallen body like a butterfly. Jim was grinning as he walked to the hill. "And that"—he tossed back over his shoulder —"that's just her *first* flight."

5

"If a bird fall, it is like being
able to bring back a token from
a dream."

—Vance Bourjaily

THE MONTANA FALCONER has been driving all day, wrestling his four-wheeler pickup along cattle tracks that lead no-where. His tireless pointers range ahead. It is late October, time to head south. Last night the thermometer dipped to ten above zero. The mountains that frame the horizon are white, their heads lost in the clouds. The remnants of an early snowfall linger under every clump of brush, and the whole world smells of sage and wet snow. But the falconer wants one more chance at a sage cock. It is his gyr-peregrine hybrid's first year. Although she has knocked down a couple of sharptails and two or three pheasants, she hasn't yet killed a big sage grouse. She will hit the monsters hard enough, but she insists on following them down. On the ground with a terrestrial bird she is at a disadvantage; invariably, the bigger bird manages to get into the air and away. But maybe this time, if he finds grouse—he hasn't seen any in two days—she will connect.

His musing cuts off as he sees his ancient pointer standing like a stone monument, nose to the wind. The pup, a novice like the bird, is honoring perfectly for once. And out here in the high sage, far from draws or timber, it has *got* to be sage grouse.

He flicks on his receiver for the fifth time since he left his teepee camp. The measured "beep-beep-beep" of the transmitter is the sound of reassurance, however incongruous on the high plains. It juts from the bird's fluffed belly feather where her leg

tucks up, attacked by a "bewit" or leather bell strap, looking like a plastic cigarette filter with a silvery twist of trailing antenna. Unlike some ultramodern falconers he still uses two bells, preferring to save the transmitter for long searches and the bells for

close-in detection. He slings a folding antenna on his back, hooks the heavy receiver to his belt; then pulls on his gauntlet and presses the gloved hand against the back of the bird's legs. She steps aboard, tightening her feathers, lowering her head. He climbs from the truck and stands still for a moment, trembling with anticipation. Takes the braces of the hood in his teeth, pulls on the far ones with his ungloved right hand, and pops the hood off.

Sometimes a hawk will stand and bob and stare, almost rouse and not rouse, mute and bob, look around and bob and stare and drive you mad, while all the time the game is creeping away. But not this afternoon. As if she knew time was getting short, she rouses, rows, and hurtles into the air with a burst of power. She burns downwind with a gyrfalcon's matchless level speed, then turns momentum into lift as she cuts back upwind. The falconer wills himself not to move, to wait until she attains a decent pitch. In what seems like hours but is more like a minute, she swings in upwind at several hundred fet. She looks ready. He knows she might get a little higher, but he can't stand the suspense. He runs in yelling, all the day's tension released.

With almost no warning thirty birds thunder up out of the sage. The six-pound cocks look like turkeys, with their long wings spread wider than his arms can reach. More and more lumber into the air, starting slowly, wobbling, then pulling away with ease. Startled, he loses track of his bird for a moment, then sees her straighten out behind an immense male and smash it. It falls, rolling and yawing and tumbling through the air, shedding feathers like a ruptured pillow, and lands in the brush looking as dead as a rock. But the falconer doesn't count sage grouse down any more until they are eaten. He runs in again, hollering with what is left of his breath, crossing the dogs who have lost their minds and manners entirely and run madly about, barking and porpoising as the flock sweeps away. The hawk swings back, looking at the ground.

And the cock leaps into the air, resurrected, crosses the startled falcon's path, and heads for the horizon like a scared canvasback. It seems impossible for anything to sustain such a strike and live, but he seems unshaken, rocking from side to side in characteristic sage-grouse motion. He's not even flying low as injured grouse often do.

And the damn-fool hawk turns around and chases him until they turn into two dots and vanish into the gray sky.

The falconer feels sick. He starts to run for the horizon, catches himself, and turns on the receiver. He unfolds the antenna and, holding it by its wooden handle, sweeps it first across the horizon, then vertically, then horizontally again on a higher line. The "beep" is strong but fluctuating; the bird is flying. He thinks for a moment, debating whether to walk or drive. The topo map shows another cattle road heading north. He knows she might fly ten miles. Sighing, he attaches the "omni" antenna to his roof by its magnetic base and slings the earphones around his neck. *If* she stays high, *if* she doesn't kill, *if* she doesn't go off hunting on her own, he may pick her up before nightfall.

H UNDREDS OF MILES south and two months later, a friend of the first falconer leans against a land cruiser parked in prairie grassland near the edge of a cultivated field. It is a half hour before sunset. On the back of his seat perches an old female peregrine, hooded, composed, waiting. The slanting rays of the sun touch her pinkish breast feathers with orange gold.

For twenty minutes, birds—lesser prairie chickens—have been dropping into the field like ducks to a marsh. The falconer thinks that probably he should have made his move already—it is getting late, and, besides, too many targets can confuse even the most experienced hawk. But after three years the strangeness of the late afternoon flight still has not lost its fascination. You can search an area of a thousand square miles, with the perfect combination of wild grassland/cultivated edge, with shinnery oak and water, and never see a grouse. Yet once you find them, they come into the same place every day, like clockwork.

He throws away the remnants of his coffee, tosses the plastic cup into the car, steps the bird to his hand, removes her leash, checks her transmitter, and unhoods her. She looks around, bobbing her head, seemingly in no hurry to go. Starts to rouse. Closes her feathers. Looks around again. Slowly expands. Rouses deliberately, mutes, rows the air, and springs.

The grouse have vanished so perfectly that it is hard to

believe they were ever there. The silence is broken only by the hiss of wind in the grass, and the tinkle of the falcon's bells. She circles and climbs, all business, until she resembles a swallow hanging in the cold air. The falconer, his pose of detachment held long enough, begins to jog, his breath coming short from the adrenalin pumping into his limbs, his heart hammering...

And an acre of grain turns into a hundred chuckling, cackling birds, leaping into the air as singles, doubles, groups of ten and more. For a moment the falconer is certain that even his old bird will miss, will be blinded by the necessity of making a choice amidst so many possibilities. The barred breasts of the prairie chickens shine gold in the evening light. He looks about desperately for the falcon and sees her flying down hard, accelerating ahead of gravity. Last year she still fell vertically toward the grouse in a classic peregrine's stoop, but as soon as she leveled off the grouse would leave her behind as if she were carrying lead weights. Now she slants, leads like a shotgunner, and *flies* straight into her prey. Even after she connects she doesn't do the usual smash-and-pass but instead grabs hold of the bird and pushes it along her line of flight. Instead of disengaging she continues to fly, skimming the grass like some grotesque four-winged creature until she disappears over an almost-invisible rise. The falconer waits a moment, but nothing appears over the horizon. He takes one last look toward the east, where the flock is no more than a flicker against the darkening sky, then begins to jog to where his bird vanished.

Ten minutes later he is worried. He thinks he has reached the right spot, but he is not sure. Could she have turned behind the little rise? Did the grouse get away? What if the hawk has gone off on her own? He is sure—well, almost sure—that neither bird could have risen above the horizon without his hyperactive senses catching them, but, damn, it's getting dark. He reaches for the telemetry switch.

Then... was that a bell? He swings his head from side to

side, mouth open, straining to quiet his breathing. He again considers turning on the receiver, but this close in, the "beep" might drown the sound of the bell. He hears it again, a faint tinkle, almost lost in the breeze. He looks for blowing feathers. Nothing. He takes another five steps, trying to walk silently...

And there she is, twenty feet to his left, shadowed by a tussock. Calm, silent, watching him, a feather in her beak.

She is standing on a prairie chicken, a pinnated grouse, loveliest and fastest of all the wild plains game. Its headdress of black plumes splays out over the snow. It is as perfect as the peregrine.

TODAY'S GROUSE circuit may feature the best hawking ever, but despite its vast geographical dimensions—from Montana in the north to Texas's Llanos Estacados in the south, from

Idaho in the west to western Minnesota, Nebraska, and central Oklahoma in the east—the grouse camps are as hard to find as the elusive prairie birds themselves. Nobody will tell you where and when to go. The four quarry species—sharptail, greater and lesser prairie chicken, and the mighty sage grouse—are all birds that crave undisturbed plains habitat, a commodity that grows rarer every year. You must make your preparations early, study vegetation and topo maps and local rainfall. And you still might not find them.

Grouse hawks are just as hard to come by. A big female prairie might do for "chickens" and sharptails, but gyrs and gyr-peregrines, plus perhaps the biggest Peale's-race peregrine females, are the only falcons big enough to fly safely at sage grouse. A good female prairie that had occasionally been flown at sage grouse killed herself stooping one two years ago. Such hawks come only from breeding projects or the arctic, and they are not handed out lightly.

There are about thirty men who go in grand style after prairie grouse every fall. These people range in age from thirty to at most fifty, have four-wheel-drive pickups, Airstream trailers (or for the very hardy, plains Indian teepees), fine English or German pointers of impeccable field trial bloodlines, .357 magnums loaded with snake shot against rattlers, and either a lot of money or a lot of time. They start in Montana or Idaho in September, end up in New Mexico or Texas by January. They care about nothing else but falconry, and their own *haut* brand of falconry at that; you could say of any one of them, as Thomas McGuane said about another kind of sporting fanatic, "This would be a man who has ruined his life for sport."

If the grouse hawker's sport sounds like merely a version of Jim's training camp plus wild birds, consider a few realities. The biggest is that, even once you know something about habitat, you may search for days or even weeks without seeing a single

grouse. You might see plenty of ducks and pheasant, but a hard-core grouse hawker scorns such "easy" birds. Some even avoid pheasants, fearing that they might lower the bird's pitch. The wind never stops, and the cold can be polar. Idaho's Charles Schwartz once told me of a time when he kept the cookstove going constantly day and night to keep from freezing in his trailer. It was fifteen degrees below zero for ten days straight, but he mourned when he had to go back to his city job and "hawking pheasants off phone poles." (Charlie doesn't go to that job any more. Just about a year ago he ceased being a chemist in Pocatello and became a professional falcon-breeding advisor to the Sheik of Bahrein.)

Other falconers have been known to complain about those who go to grouse camp, calling them snobbish, arrogant, self-styled aristocrats, rich bastards, and worse. There is perhaps a grain of truth in some of these charges. The grouse hawkers avoid publicity to the point of avoiding human beings, especially other (nongrouse) falconers. Like all falconers they are basically self-made, having worked up to their precious gyrs through years of more common hawks; like all self-made men, they want others to pay their dues. As for money, it doesn't hurt to be wealthy if you want to take two or more months off in the fall, though there are more than a couple of men of modest means on the high plains who make great sacrifices to be there. As for arrogance, a little of the bird's attitude rubs off on anyone who flies a hawk for a while, be it a gyrfalcon or a redtail. You know that most people in this or any other civilization wouldn't put that much time or discipline into anything, much less into training a bird.

But the biggest difference between those who drive the circuit from Montana to New Mexico every year and almost anybody else is just an extra measure of dedication, of a fanatic ability to focus, of a willingness to be lonely in order to experience the finest hawking of all time. If these are aristocrats they are an aristocracy of merit rather than privilege, with the open public range instead of inherited estates, with the unmanageable and civilization-avoiding sage grouse rather than the cultivated pheasant as their quarry. They work overtime all year; then some travel from as far as New York to be in the big back country with their birds. Is it any wonder that they might describe their ideal scene as, in the words of the Peregrine Fund's Jim Weaver: "BLM land, good water, fantastic scenery . . . and best of all, no people."

OF COURSE, not all good hawking is so expensive or falcon-arrogant. If you want to see a perfect miniature of a gyr's flight, but one you can indulge in on the beach or in a park, try a merlin. You should be able to have it in the air within two weeks of its capture, and it will attempt to catch almost anything. Though it rarely goes up high, it will stick to its prey as though magnetized, performing short twisting stoops and climbing sharply under full power. Of course, unless you fly it on the beach, your surroundings may not be so romantic. One of the best merlin flights I ever saw was after a starling. The quarry evaded four stoops and then disappeared behind a belt of trees. When we emerged neither bird was in sight. Ten minutes later and well up the road we heard a commotion of sparrows behind one of those ubiquitous fast-food stands that line the roads. I finally figured out that the frenzy centered on a dumpster. When I peered over the edge I beheld the five-ounce perfect predator, all gun-metal blue elegance, pulling feathers from the starling atop a mound of crumpled yellow paper and styrofoam. He looked quite at home.

Or perhaps you like bigger game, want to be able to take advantage of the variety of prey species, from smaller birds to snowshoe hares, that live tolerantly close to man. Then you'd best try a goshawk, or, in a warm climate, a Harris's. If you can put up with a gos, the rewards are great and the excitement continuous. Gosses can take quail, crows, squirrels, pheasant, rabbit, woodcock, starling, duck—and occasionally, against your intentions, stray cats, green herons, marsh hawks, and even wild gosses. My friend Mark was out one winter after snowshoes when his gos disappeared into an alder thicket, from which erupted a cacophony of goshawk noise. He ran in to find his female passager locked toe-to-toe with a beautiful blue haggard. As he had a bird-bander friend, he decided to take it home. He disentangled the combatants and distracted his own bird with a hunk of pigeon on her lure, then tucked the newcomer head-down into his hawking bag, where only her barred tail tip protruded.

All went well until, about to get into his car, he was spotted by a woman he knew with a group of birders in tow. She introduced them and they duly admired the yellow-eyed monster. Then one of them noticed the tail-tip and spoke up timidly:

"Is that where you keep your spare?"

Idiot encounters, spookiness, unintentional game violations, and scarred hands aside, nothing is more effective than the *cuisinier*. Ralph Buscemi took ninety-six very mixed head of game one year with a goshawk, and every one was exciting. But it is a brand of excitement different from the kind you get in a wide open plains flight with its high visibility and ecstatic stoops. Often when flying a gos you never even see the strike or the kill, though you are just as plugged in. You stand in an opening in the alders, ears straining, hearing the bells circle. And if you are very lucky a hare, a lump of snow with eyes, will pass making ten-foot bounds, straining flat out with the gos like old gray death rowing along behind it. And sometimes she will roll it over, and sometimes it will disappear again while you wait for the jangle and cry

that signify a kill or the dead silence that might mean a miss and might mean a lost hawk.

Betsy's first exposure to this kind of hawking made falconry for her. We were out with Ralph Buscemi after cottontails, using a first-year male gos, hunting over waist-high brush. We would start a rabbit, sometimes seeing a puff of white hair, most often nothing at all. The gos would launch from Ralph's fist and fly the rabbit's course over the bushes, turning, doubling, hovering stopped-dead in the air, then cutting back on the same track at an impossible angle in perfect mirror image of his quarry's run. Sometimes he would crash to earth, but the brush that day was too thick for the bird to force his way through. Even so, despite his lack of "success" and despite the freezing drizzle that finally made us all too wet to continue, it was a dazzling exhibition of a goshawk's skill.

I FLY MOSTLY longwings these days. I have a stylish quail hawk who waits on as precisely as a flown kite, who can stoop to the lure fifty times before he begins to pant, who is as tame and affectionate as a cocker spaniel. But the single day's hawking I remember best was that seven-rabbit day with my plebeian old redtail. I don't know exactly why. Maybe it was the glory of that hunt in contrast to life at the time, which was a sour twentieth-century mix of breakup and misunderstanding, unemployment and confusion of goals. Or maybe it was that the day contained everything that falconry should: beauty, cold, adrenalin, cama-raderie, exertion, trust between bird and man, clean savagery, and happy exhaustion. I remember it in a series of focused moments, unfading mental snapshots more vivid than any photographs.

Fɪʀsᴛ: an expanse of eye-dazzling white, two feet of new
snow covering the industrial "park" wasteland's debris and
weeds, making it almost beautiful. I am standing on a mound at
the edge, stomping to test my snowshoes, drinking in the air.
Cinnamon balances peevishly on my fist, spreading his wings,
standing first on one foot, then on the other, tugging. He wants
to fly.

A ꜰᴇᴡ ᴍɪɴᴜᴛᴇs later. We have spotted a rabbit a couple of
hundred yards away, a dot under a forsaken apple tree.
Cinnamon stands atop another tree, fifty yards from the rabbit,
neck extended, peering. We are circling to flush it toward him.
And it breaks!

TWO FLUSHES later now: rabbits two, falconers nothing. An unseen cottontail bounds toward us, kicking up puffs of powder snow like smoke. And behind it, head-on toward us so he looks like a shallow "V" or stylized sea gull in a kid's painting, comes Cinnamon stroking hard. Our eyes cannot distinguish the strike; we just see a confusion of snow and motion that settles into one hawk, mantling, talons extended and buried in a quivering rabbit's head. One!

CINNAMON has a rabbit pinned down beneath an upended stump. John roots around under it and the bunny breaks, straight into my hands. For the snapshot I hold it quivering in my hands, beyond amazement. I convulsively throw it away from me; then, after it takes three hard jumps, remember to "HO HAWK!" Cinnamon chases it over a hilltop, but when I run up he is sitting in a tree.

CINNAMON has killed two more rabbits now and is feeling a little disgruntled at our having taken them away. I stop at the edge of a twenty-foot cutbank and let him fly to a tree. Tom and John unearth a rabbit from a brush pile below me, but Cinnamon turns his back, pointedly ignoring it. I slide down, sitting on my snowshoes, and call him in for a reward of rabbit heart and pigeon breast. "Lunch break?"

WE ARE SITTING in the cab of Tom's truck in a McBurger's parking lot. I am on the window side. Cinnamon sits on my knee, pulling at a fleshless but entertaining rabbit's foot, appeased and content. Two teenaged girls stop in amazement as his head rises above the dashboard. "Oh, where did you get him, he's byooteeful!" Then they see the rabbit fur. "Ohmygod, what's that, that's *horrible*, how can you *do* it, it's so *GROSS!*" I smile, momentarily a little embarrassed, and say nothing. There is no talking to most urban and suburban kids about hunting these days. They have been brought up on the "Grizzly Adams" school of nature study, beside which even Disney's notorious fables resemble *True Life Adventures*.

L ATE AFTERNOON. We are in the field again, with an unheard-of six rabbits in the bag, trying like humans for an excess above anything an avian predator would dream of. I stand on a stump, hand held high above my head, Cin perched on my knuckles, while John and Tom probe another brush pile. A rabbit starts out between Tom's feet; Cinnamon leaves my glove and hurtles after it. As he turns and falls, heavy as a fist, it turns and breaks back straight toward us. The hawk hits the ground, flings out a wing for balance, runs along the ground until he is airborne, and gives chase. Seeing us standing in front of him, the rabbit veers toward open ground. It is his last mistake, for in a sudden goshawklike burst of speed Cinnamon overtakes him and enfolds him in his wings. The rabbit's startled squall cuts off before we reach the kill, and the hawk's great head comes up. I lift him together with the limp bunny, comforting, saying, "This one's all yours, old buddy . . ." And he looks me in the eye and foots me, hard, his hind talon penetrating through the rabbit skin and to the bone in my thumb. Saying, perhaps, "Damn straight it's mine!"

H OMEWARD BOUND, in the dark. Cin sits on my knee again, sleepy and gorged, his crop the size of a grapefruit. A melancholy Bonnie Raitt blues plays on the radio. I hum along, tickle the hawk's belly feathers, at peace with the world. From time to time Tom pounds the steering wheel with his hand and exclaims aloud at some moment of the already dreamlike day: "Did you *see* it when he rolled that one? In*cred*ible!" And it is incredible. Here, at the very edge of the city, it seems we have found a way of going on, of touching the wild in this twentieth century.

CODA

"The way back cannot be the same for all of
us, but for those like myself it means a
descent of the rungs until we stand again
amid the other creatures of the earth and
share to some small extent their vision of it"
—Gavin Maxwell

Now you have lived through the stages of becoming a
falconer. You have started with the beauty of the birds, the
fascination of their habits, and been moved by that contradictory
impulse to possess them and to release them to freedom. You
have caught a bird, experiencing all the fun and fascination of
outwitting an alien species. You have tested your commitment in
the suffering and frustration you must go through to forge the
bond. And you have received your reward in the return of a
free-hunting bird to your fist. So where do we go from here?
What is our future in the "Ancient Occupation?"

Some falconers fear, and many of our opponents hope, that
falconry is a dying sport. Persistent pesticides and habitat de-
struction have endangered some populations of wild hawks,
though most have shown an amazing ability to rebound if we
allow them to. Still, extreme "hands-off" environmentalists
have always held a peculiar hatred of falconry, an attitude rooted
more in quasi-theological belief than in biological realities.
Falcons somehow generate more passion than most animals (cf.
King James I), and those who think that mere bird-banding is
immoral interference with the wild can hardly be expected to

tolerate the manipulations inherent in falconry. These are the same people who would rather allow the California condor to become extinct than to preserve it by captive breeding; the ones who oppose the reintroduction of the peregrine because the released birds ("Cornell chickens") are of mixed race instead of pure *anatum*. The proper reply to all these arguments is the obvious one, that falconers have *never* endangered a single species of raptor, never in all recorded history.

"Commercialization" is another can of worms, an issue that pits falconer against falconer ("an extreme stirrer-up of passions"). Some breeders are supposed to be stockpiling birds in order to make a great financial killing selling them to "the Arabs" when and if legal sales are allowed. But ten-thousand-dollar peregrines have probably never been more than the paranoid fancies of a few federal wildlife agents. The Arabs can buy peregrines elsewhere at prices equivalent to the cost of good purebred dogs or cheap horses. Besides, you could argue that legalizing sales of captive-bred birds would drive down the alleged black-market prices, as well as taking pressure off wild eyries.

Looking at the situation realistically, it might be easier to see the first new domestication in eons. Third-generation birds are now a commonplace, and raptor stud books exist. Birds of the genus *Falco* seem to have the ability to make fertile interspecies hybrids that also characterizes *Canis*, the genus of wolf and domestic dog.

Which doesn't mean that our grandchildren will see a hawk in every backyard. Falconry requires a feeling for the woods and fields, an intuitive grasp of ecology, both rare in this plastic age. Its practitioners are individualistic to the point of anarchism, committed to the point of obsession, and as proud as their birds. Although they are sometimes paranoid, they as often have reason. To be a serious falconer a person must be a mixture of predator and St. Francis, with all the masochistic self-discipline of a Zen student. There will never be more than a few such people.

But there will always be those few, regardless of law or custom, as long as the birds and the human race exist. We must all try to preserve the great public lands of the West, where falconry has reached a new zenith. But even deep in our civilization, pheasants haunt industrial parks and urban cemeteries; doves feed in vacant lots, and rabbits run in the forgotten places beside our highways. Hawks hunt there, with us or without us. Goshawks bounce off trail bikers' helmets, and peregrines haunt our skyscrapers.

Let me leave you one last untaken snapshot from that day of industrial hawking. Another redtail, a big new-caught female, bends over her kill, a rabbit dislodged from a machine-age brush pile made of I beams. The sun is setting, staining the snow a deep golden red. Only four figures are there—three human hunters and the mingled form of hawk and prey, black against the bloody sky. The humans wear fur-edged parkas. Two stand silently by on snowshoes; the third kneels beside the hawk, cutting the rabbit open to reward the bird. His cloud of breath mingles with the rush of steam from the rabbit's body cavity and floats downwind. The hawk bows and eats.

There is no way to tell where or when this picture comes from, not on three continents, not in four thousand years.

Falconry lives.

REFERENCES

(A complete falconry bibliography is beyond
the scope of this book. These are works that
I have quoted or used directly.)

Allen, Mark. *Falconry in Arabia*. London: Orbis, 1980. A fine book, as much about falconers as about hawks.

Beebe, Frank. *Hawks, Falcons and Falconry*. Saanichton, British Columbia, Canada: Hancock House, 1976. Best basic book, with some eccentric ideas.

Bert, Edmund. *An Approved Treatise on Hawkes and Hawking*. 1619. Reprint. Trowbridge, England: Thames Valley Press, 1973.

Bourjaily, Vance. *The Unnatural Enemy*. New York: Dial, 1963.

Cade, Tom J.. *The Falcons of the World*. Ithaca: Cornell University Press/Comstock, 1982. The definitive word on falcon biology.

Falconer, The. Journal of the British Falconers Club, 1937–1971. Saskatoon, Saskatchewan, Canada: Falconiforme Press, 1978.

Ford, Emma. *Falconry in Mews and Field*. London: Batsford, 1982. A decidedly untraditional English book with very good material on shortwings, equipment, and breeding.

Glasier, Philip. *Falconry and Hawking*. Newton, Mass.: Charles Branford, 1979.

Hamerstrom, Frances. *An Eagle to the Sky*. Iowa City, Iowa: Iowa University Press, 1970.

Jeffers, Robinson. *Selected Poems*. New York: Vintage, 1963.

Leahy, Christopher. *The Birdwatcher's Companion*. New York: Hill and Wang, 1982. Encyclopedic. Good entry on falconry.

Leopold, Aldo. *A Sand County Almanac*. New York and London: Oxford University Press, 1966.

Longrigg, Roger. *The English Squire and His Sport*. New York: St. Martin's Press, 1977.

Lorenz, Konrad. *King Solomon's Ring*. New York: Thomas Y. Crowell, 1952.

McElroy, Harry. *Desert Hawking II*. Privately printed, 1977. Original book on accipiters, not just for the desert.

Mavrogordato, J. G. *A Hawk for the Bush*. Witherby, 1960; reprinted by Clarkson N. Potter (no date).
———*A Falcon for the Field*. London: Knightly Vernon, 1966. The best texts ever, with fine illustrations, by a falconer who can write. English but not hidebound.

Maxwell, Gavin. *Raven Seek Thy Brother*. New York: Dutton, 1969.

Meinertzhagen, Richard. *Birds of Arabia*. Edinburgh: Oliver & Boyd, 1954.
———*Pirates and Predators*. Edinburgh: Oliver & Boyd, 1959.

Michell, E. B. *The Art and Practice of Hawking*. 1900. Reprint. Newton, Mass.: Charles Branford, 1959. Classic English text.

Stevens, Ronald. *Laggard*. Winchester, Mass.: Faber & Faber, 1953.

———*Observations on Modern Falconry*. Privately printed, 1957. Indispensable.

Taylor, Rod. *Florida East Coast Champion*. San Francisco: Straight Arrow, 1972.

Terres, John K. *The Audubon Society Encyclopedia of North American Birds*. New York: Knopf, 1980.

White, T. H. *England Have My Bones*. 1936. Reprint. New York: G. P. Putnam's, 1982. *The Goshawk*. Jonathan Cape. Reprint. New York: The Viking Press, 1971. *The White/Garnett Letters*, New York: The Viking Press, 1968. Falconers often dislike *The Goshawk* because White admits his ineptitude; still, it is the only book to give you the *feel* of manning a hawk.